Emily Bronte

and

German Romanticism

Maggie Allen

CONTENTS

INTRODUCTION

Emily Bronte was born in England July 31st 1818, when England was undergoing great upheavals and advancements in all areas of life. To consider the works of Emily Brontë and the German Romantics it is necessary to understand the context of the period in which they were writing and those elements which were influential.

The Romantic period had been well established in Europe since the late eighteenth century, when Europe had been on the verge of new beginnings following the wars and political doctrines of earlier times. As science, technology and industry forged ahead, the intellectual movements also felt the winds of change blowing over them, as artists of all genres began to break free of the old classical models in favour of a more creative and imaginative output. They were no longer confined to the rigid systems of the past, but were free to pen their thoughts and develop their own distinctive styles. Women writers also emerged to challenge and confront their male counterparts.

The end of the French Revolution saw an explosion of relief as artists of all genres could finally give way to more freedom of expression. This dynamic outpouring touched the entire European Continent. But in literature there were individual differences, as there are in cultures and languages. Different histories have always reflected their own society, culture and beliefs, but the close of the eighteenth century saw a new beginning as people began to feel, act and react in a much more universal way. On the political front both the Government and its people in England were still talking and reflecting upon the events of the French Revolution and its aftermath.

Such discussions promoted a new type of intellectual development in the areas of literary and philosophical enquiry. The new generation found they had more leisure time than their predecessors. It was not long before the country found itself with many emerging authors and poets, who brought with them a new freedom of imagination. Madame de Stael was author of several works of fiction and non-fiction, and was recognised in England for her popular novels *Delphine* (1803), and *Corrine* (1807). But it was her literary and social analysis which people were interested in. She stated that "the English are great writers in verse, and carry eloquence of mind to the highest degree; but their works in prose scarcely partake of that life and energy which are found in their poetry [and because] it has more often been employed in commercial affairs than in literature, it has never been displayed in all its shades of variety."[1]

She concluded that the English philosophy [was] more scientific and "seems as if the English feared to give too much scope to their fancy, except in their poetic inspiration: when they write in prose a sort of modesty or bashfulness seems to keep their sentiments in captivity."[2] The characteristics she referred to was the familiar conservative 'stiff-upper lip' of the English, which they were often accused of. However, what followed such observations was the grasping of the imagination by poets and writers alike as Romanticism swept into England. The term of Romanticism had always been elusive, with critics and academics attempting to thrash out a definition, and was one of those grey areas which could never receive a full definition, but could be classified as having several distinctive traits in which to recognise such work. Romanticism, in its broadest sense, was a search for truth. It was a movement, a reaction to the past, to oppressions and wars, confinements and prejudice, allowing the individual to become aware of himself and his own mortality, to make his own choices, and most of all to give free reign to the emotions. It was after all an opposing product of previous social and cultural revolutions. In such a sense it could be argued that Romanticism was that which happened at a certain time in history, in a certain place and to certain individuals. It was, in that respect, confined to a certain place and time. Authors and critics have sought to define the term 'Romanticism,' over the years and have offered many alternatives. Romanticism could also be described as a 'function,' rather than having a particular dictionary definition, with its most outstanding function being freedom of expression; writers and poets could question and display their thoughts and emotions through their works. The overall function of Romanticism that writers and poets agreed upon seemed to be the quest to find man's place in society and the universe.

English poets and writers were influenced by the movement, and began to look around them noticing as though for the first time, the beauty and wonder of nature. Which, in turn, led them to question God, their beliefs and own mortality. Further, it was a reaction to the newly emerging industrial landscape in and around the cities, which prompted the vision of artists, poets and writers to escape to the natural surroundings of the countryside.

Emily Brontë's poetry and her further prose work *Wuthering Heights* were later, but clear examples of Romanticism. A comparison of the style, structure and subject matter of the poems and other works by Emily Brontë and the German Romantic authors demonstrated how their different cultural ethos brought them towards a spiritual and mystical union. Mrs Humphrey Ward commented that "the source of *Wuthering Heights* had probably come from *The Tales of Hoffmann*. It is perhaps more artistically true to suppose it had its origins in Emily 's own untamed spirit, for as a piece of literature it stands alone in its vehemence, its intensity, and in what Swinbourne called 'the dark unconscious instinct of nature worship that streaked her passionate genius.'"[3]

The Romantic Movement taking place throughout Europe was not a single but multiple movement, "the timing and form differed from one country to another because it was in each case determined by the literary background as well as by social and political factors."[4]

Carlyle wrote about the reception of German literature growing in England with an expanding sense of assuredness, "because it grounds itself on better knowledge, on direct style and judgement. Within the last ten years independent German readers have increased a hundredfold…we regard this revival of our intercourse after twenty years of languor or suspension as among the most remarkable and even promising feature of our recent intellectual history."[5]

Such energetic comments would have sown the seeds of interest in an independent mind such as Emily's, seeds that would blossom and mirror German inspiration. Her solitary life "as she looked on the moors, absorbing all they gave her...they alone saw her meditations of solitude...the wind playing around her was her companion; the light fading before her was all she asked for solace when her day's work was done."[6]

Emily's world shared many interests of the German Romantics in which she had "visions of something, as yet indistinct, rising with bold outlines from the grim landscape above factories and streets obscured by smoke...the shapes disclosed had challenged her to penetrate its mystery."[7]

A. Mary F. Robinson stated that there were three influences in the works of Emily Brontë, the first being her own surroundings; her character; and her own experiences, but added that a fourth "cannot be omitted, and that was the influence of German literature –especially with Hoffmann's tales." She continued "In Emily's day, Romance and Germany had one significance; it is true that in London and in prose the German influence was dying out, but in distant Haworth, and in the writings of such poets as Emily would read...it is still predominant."[8] As both Mrs Gaskell and A. Mary F. Robinson pointed out, "Emily in the midst of her business at Haworth [could be seen] reading her German book at night, as she sits on the hearthrug with her arm around Keeper's neck...the study of German [was] an influence that entered her mind and helped to shape the fashion of her thoughts."[9]

Robert K. Wallace commented about Emily's European experience in Brussels which "has been overlooked by too many students of this period in her life in which she discovered a world of cathedrals and pictures, learned to read the masters of French and German literature, "all of which [helped her to] produce some of the best work of her life, indicating that her foreign experience was to provide a turning point in her life."[10] Mrs Humphrey Ward also commented upon Emily's European trip stating that "it represented the grafting of a European- and specifically German- tradition upon a mind already richly stored with English and local reality."[11]

Mrs Ward continued to comment upon how "Emily worked probably under influences from German literature. We know that the Brontes read *Blackwood's* diligently...*Blackwood's* published about 1839 certain translations including Tieck's *Pietro d' Abano*...also Goethe's *Dichtung und Wahrheit*..."[12]

This investigation has concentrated upon that influence, dealing with the broader cultural background to Emily 's life and work and how her surroundings provided her with inspiration, drawing her into a world of imagination which she expressed in her poetry, and how that world had its parallel with the German Romantic poets. Further analyses charted the development of the Romantic Movement in Germany, its spread of popularity in Europe and subsequent arrival in England, and how it explored German beliefs and techniques including the Gothic, a darker element and expression of Romanticism.

According to Rictor Norton "the Gothic created a literary revolution as the novel in Sir Walter Scott's words, "flew from hand to hand among middle-class tradespeople and their daughters, working-class men, ladies' maids, university students and professors, earls and gentlewomen."[13]

The Gothic was not just limited to literature, as between 1800 and 1820 a flood of pamphlets displayed the craze for Gothic architecture. The German movement had brought with it an overwhelming influence which affected many aspects of daily life, even country clergymen were cleaning and restoring their churches, and a few, like Tennyson's father carried their enthusiasm into their homes, adorning their churches with Gothic detail."[14]

In a more specific historical sense, Gothic was associated with the history of the northern Germanic nations whose fierce avowal of the values of freedom and democracy was claimed as an ancient heritage."[15] Although Gothic architecture was so popular, it was literature which held a sustained appeal, especially in the period dominated by Romanticism, where the individual became "alienated from society and themselves…the wanderer encounters the new form of the Gothic ghost or double shadow of himself."[16]

In the poetry of Emily Bronte the main themes had been initially inspired by the Bronte children's *'Gondal'* adventures. Themes of her more mature poetry centred upon the spiritual imagination, nature, God, - and frequently the dramatic use of music which would infiltrate those areas.

Those main important sections highlighted the effects of Romanticism, Gothicism, Europe and the influence of the German Romantic poets in their style, techniques and subject matter. The female as writer and poet of Romanticism and the Gothic, had been ignored over the years, as the emphasis has always been male-dominated, due to its inception by the Jena male group of philosophers and writers in Germany, and in England by poets Wordsworth, Coleridge, Crabbe and Shelley. Women had struggled to become recognised as writers and poets, even the females; Anne, Emily and Charlotte, had given themselves false names to mislead the publishers, being known as Acton, Ellis and Currer Bell. It was a ploy destined for success.

The women writers and poets in both England and Germany, from the late eighteen hundreds to the mid nineteenth century had taken up the challenge and penned their own thoughts and ideas. It was interesting to note the similarities and ideas of the German female writer, the English female writer and Emily Bronte. Despite the geographical distance between them, the Romantic and Gothic could be charted throughout their poems, drama and fiction, and whilst no simple definitive factor linked Emily directly to the German poets, the overwhelming suggestion is that the cumulative effect of Romanticism has presented evidence which has been difficult to deny.

CHAPTER ONE: A Literary Background

"They were not ladies…they were not even successful as governesses, that their father and brother were a pair of reprobates, and that they themselves, being embittered by the fact that they were not admitted to the good society of their neighbourhood, had deliberately revenged themselves by writing scurrilous libels and caricatures in order to bring Yorkshire men and women into contempt."[1]

Those strong words of disapproval about the Bronte family's arrival in Haworth seem unrecognisable to the reader in the twenty-first century, but they did point to a very unique family. The environment in which they were surrounded was a cold, bleak and wild one where poverty, illness and death were everyday occurrences.

The village of "Haworth sits upon the top of a "steep hill, with a background of dun and purple moors, rising and sweeping away yet higher than the church, which is built at the very summit of the long narrow street. All around the horizon there is this same line of sinuous wave-like hills; the scoops into which they fall only revealing other hills beyond, of similar colour and shape crowned with wild, bleak moors –grand, from the ideas of solitude and loneliness which they suggest, or oppressive from the feeling which they give of being pent-up by some monotonous and illimitable barrier, according to the mood of mind in which the spectator may be."[2]

The Bronte family only had to look out of the window to see the graveyard surrounding them was a constant reminder of death and mortality. By studying the writings of the Bronte family, the reader can detect the underlying courage, morality and independence of those individuals who had been so cruelly misjudged by their own neighbours.

Elizabeth Gaskell pointed out, "There is little display of the amenities of life among this wild, rough population. Their accent is curt; their accent and tone of speech blunt and harsh."[3] she continued, "They are not emotional; they are not easily made into friends or enemies; but once lovers or haters, it is difficult to change their feelings." With regard to strangers, she stated, "They have no superior to court, no civilities to practice; a sour and sturdy humour is the consequence, so that a stranger is shocked by a tone of defiance in every voice, and an air of fierceness in every countenance. Even now, a stranger can hardly ask a question without receiving some crusty reply, if indeed, he receive any at all. Yet, if the 'foreigner' takes all this churlishness good-humouredly, or as a matter of course, and makes good any claim upon their latent kindness or hospitality, they are faithful and generous, and thoroughly to be relied upon."[4]

Frank Peel, in his article about *The History of the Spen Valley,* stated how he found Haworth in 1850 to be "the most dead-alive, melancholy- looking place it has ever been my lot to see. No sign of life, or trace of trade, or traffic was perceptible. The very houses seemed miserable, and if stones could look positively heart-broken they did...How anyone could live a lifetime there, and not grow morbid, was incomprehensible...[but when] stood in front of the parsonage, all the inner mysteries of *Wuthering Heights* and *Wildfell Hall,* and gnome-like genius and premature deaths of Ellis and Acton Bell were clear to me."[5]

Although Haworth in Yorkshire has always been associated with the 's, their father had been born in Ireland (St. Patrick's Day 1777) and their mother, Maria Branwell, originated from Cornwall. She died after only eighteen months at Haworth (1821) leaving six children in the care of their father and Aunt Elizabeth Branwell. The two elder daughters, Maria and Elizabeth also died, leaving surviving children Charlotte, Emily, Anne and Branwell.

The initial literary influence of the children can be traced down through the family of Patrick Bronte who, as a young man had worked as a weaver, usually with a book in his hand, because of his love of literature following in the footsteps of his own father, Hugh, who "had passed thro' strange experiences and could relate stories, some such as melt the heart to pity, others such as cause the flesh to creep and stir the passion for the weird and wonderful." Patrick was "possessed of the desire to learn, and love of learning is like the sea-wave, which the more you drink it the more you thirst." [6] He visited book stalls as often as he could, but his passion for reading became a distraction when weaving and he lost his job. Luck was on his side when Andrew Harshaw heard Patrick reciting lines from Milton's *Paradise Lost* and being impressed, offered him teaching work, encouraging him to keep on reading and learning.

In 1802 Patrick followed his dream and entered Cambridge University, where he received his degree and entered the ministry. The change to his life offered the opportunity for Patrick to pen his first poetic works. Endowed with a passionate love of nature he was able to express himself through his poetry, producing; *Winter Evening Thoughts* (1810) followed by *"The Cottage in the Wood*, the prose piece *The Maid of Killarney, The Irish Cabin,* and finally his *Cottage Poems."* [7]

Prior to undertaking the parish of Haworth, Patrick held the curacies of Dewsbury, Hartshead-cum-Clifton and Thornton. In those days [Haworth] was remote, secluded, aloof, far from railroad and the busy stir of life." [8] James Senior pointed out that even then the moors were the great attraction of Haworth,

"There is always fresh air on the moors; pleasant, life-giving, invigorating breezes are found there even on hot summer days, when the air is stagnant and stifling in the valleys…the moors breathe liberty. On them the thoughts go free. They fascinate; and over those who frequent them most, falls a strangely mysterious and magic spell. The moors are calling them, and they are under the charm." [9] For Emily the moors became her special place, with nature providing all the ingredients for her imagination to run free. The bleak Yorkshire surroundings also provided Charlotte and Anne with ideas for their literary endeavours, although Branwell, born a year after Charlotte in 1817, was not to be as fortunate as his sisters.

As the only son he was educated by his father; "By the age of ten Branwell had been taught ancient and modern history, Greek and Latin, and had read the works of Homer and Virgil."[10] But it was his later life of alcoholism, drug addiction and debts, coupled with his disastrous and questionable romance with Mrs Robinson, the wife of his employer, which signalled his eventual downfall.

Emily, meanwhile, had become the 'son' substitute as her father had "unbounded confidence in his daughter Emily, knowing, as he did, her unparalleled intrepidity and firmness, that he resolved to learn her to shoot. Mr. had taken pleasure in fending off his worries and frustrations by shooting at a mark. With Emily by his side they practised with pistols…he called upon her "now my dear girl, let me see how well you can shoot today [she would drop anything she was doing and]…her most winning and musical voice would be heard to ring through the house in response, 'yes, papa."[11]

All the Bronte children had, however, a thirst for literature, and as Clement Shorter stated, "these Bronte children toiled often on foot the self-same journey, bringing back books from the library of the Mechanics Institute, and thereby supplementing the scantily furnished book-shelves of their own home."[12]

Charlotte, the eldest daughter (1816) went on to successfully write both poetry and novels. Frank Peel described Charlotte as being "diminutive in height, and extremely fragile. Her hand was one of the smallest I ever grasped. She had no pretensions to being considered beautiful, and was as far removed from being plain. She had rather light brown hair, somewhat thin and drawn plainly over her brow. Her complexion had no trace of colour in it, and her lips were pallid also; but she had a most sweet smile, with a touch of true melancholy in it. Altogether she was as unpretending, undemonstrative, quiet a little lady as you would well meet. Her age I took to be about five and thirty. But when you saw and felt her eyes, the spirit that created *Jane Eyre* was revealed at once to you. They were rather small, but of very peculiar colour, and had a strong lustre and intensity. They were chameleon-like, a blending of various brown and olive tints. But they looked you through and through – and you felt they were forming an opinion of you...[into] the innermost core of your soul."[13]

Of other writers, Peel stated that although she had met Charles Dickens, "she admired his genius, but did not like him."[14] However, she "absolutely worshipped" Thackeray, regarding him as "the first social regenerator of the day...his wit is bright, his humour attractive, but both bare the same relation to his serious genius...I have alluded to Mr. Thackeray, because to him – if he will accept the tribute of a total stranger – I have dedicated this second edition of Jane Eyre."[15].

She produced the novel *Jane Eyre* (1847) which has remained one of the greatest novels of all time for its realism and social depiction of a disadvantaged child growing up in a hostile environment amongst cruel adults; the inspiration taken from her own childhood days at Cowan Bridge, followed by the death of her two younger sisters. The second part of the novel then gave an account of Jane as an adult and governess, again Charlotte had experienced life as a governess. Her introduction to Thornfield Hall, allowed Charlotte to let her imagination soar with Gothic horror, introducing the mysterious Mr Rochester and mad woman in the attic. The third part developed the love-relationship between Rochester and Jane. Charlotte 's other novels *Shirley* (1849) *Villette* (1853) and *The Professor* (1857) followed with mixed results, and finally *Emma* which was eventually completed by another writer who wished to remain anonymous. *Shirley* offered a further sociological account of the conflict between nature and industry, although the early narrative was taken up with the habits of the clergy, giving a misleading impression of the novel and plot. It did, however, radiate with tongue-in-cheek humour as Charlotte described the clergymen's selfish routines, living life in their own bubble, not realising how the people in their communities were suffering. It was a novel with two leading ladies; Shirley Keeldar and Caroline Helstone whose opposite lives and loves became entwined. Having first followed the fortunes of the feminine Caroline, the appearance of Shirley presented a much stronger character. She did not want to be left out of the unfolding action as she observed and commented upon the episodes of violence by the labourers who had lost their jobs due to industrialisation. An unexpected aspect to the plot was the introduction of Mrs Pryor who revealed herself to be Caroline's mother. The romantic theme was interwoven as Caroline and Shirley found love with brothers Robert and Louis (Gérard) Moore, ensuring a happy conclusion.

Villette was a complex novel, with a psychological and emotional content. The title name was Charlotte's own for Brussels, where she had experienced life as both student and governess. The novel examined both religious faith and human love. The characters were drawn from the people she had encountered. The character of Polly occupied the voice of reason, always calm and analytical, suggesting an influence from Emily Bronte who had accompanied Charlotte to Brussels. The character of Dr. John represented an 'ideal,' as he was always described in glowing terms by all who knew him. There was no background information about the main female character of Lucy Snow, but her independent spirit and cold exterior suggested an intelligence and intellect, combined with spiritual and emotional bravery. Although her name suggested a cool exterior, inside Lucy was fragile, emotional and vulnerable. Her innermost thoughts, her pain and anguish surrounding her situation in the school and were embedded strongly throughout the novel. Gothic elements added to the atmosphere with the appearance of the spectral nun, Justine-Marie. The abundance of psychoanalytical searching led to a form of nervous breakdown, and led her to the confessional in the Catholic Church. Despite the loneliness and spiritual vacuum she found herself in, as Protestantism crossed swords with Catholicism, Lucy's strength of character sustained her and led towards a calm acceptance that she must look forward and plan her future. The novel ended not quite complete; no relationship with Mm. Paul, who had vanished from her life suddenly, but his legacy of a house and school for Lucy meant she could move forward with her plans for her future life. Despite the lack of the usual happy ending, the novel concluded on a hopeful and optimistic note.

The Professor was also set in Brussels, although having a male main character, William Crimsworth, as the tutor. The novel followed his journey from the hostile relationship with his brother in England to a new life in Brussels. The novel, despite being short, was quite a literary affair as Charlotte Bronte chose an extensive use of French/Flemish language. It was also interesting to note the mention of French and German authors who occupied their position on the bookshelves of Mr. Hunsden, including Goethe, Schiller and Jean Paul Richter. Those authors had been popular in England and would also have been found on the bookshelves of the Bronte household.

The Professor concentrated upon life in the school, the characters of his pupils and, further, his relationship with Mdlle. Frances Henri, who he eventually married, and moved back to England. In conclusion, the message of the novel was one about work and survival.

Finally, the novel *Emma* was a complete departure from the norm, containing a realism which had found its way into the modern novel in the late nineteenth century. *Emma* could be described as a detective novel with its mixture of mystery and suspense, and that the 'Emma' in question would turn out to be the child Martina, and not the villain of the piece, who turned out to be the step-daughter. Chasing after clues around the country kept the reader gripped. The novel was completed after the death of Charlotte Bronte by a lady writer who has remained anonymous. The result was a complete success. Although we had no idea of how Charlotte would have developed her novel, she would have been pleased with the outcome, the conclusion was true to style as the family came together and even the villain was forgiven, as the female character of Arminet married her 'detective' Mr. Ellin, and gave birth to a daughter naming her Emma.

Anne Bronte (1820) has been remembered for her novels *Agnes Grey*, and *The Tenant of Wildfell Hall*. George Smith recalled Anne Bronte as "a quiet, rather subdued person, by no means pretty, yet of a pleasing appearance. Her manner was curiously expressive of a wish for protection and encouragement, a kind of constant appeal which invited sympathy.(Kathryn White's Introduction to *Agnes Grey*) Ellen Nussey described Anne as "quite different in appearance from the others...her hair was very pretty, light brown, and fell on her neck in graceful curls. She had lovely violet-blue eyes, fine pencilled eyebrows, and a clear, almost transparent complexion."[16]

Charlotte stated that her sister Anne "was milder and more subdued [than Emily's]; she wanted the power, the fire, the originality of her sister but was well-endowed with quiet virtues of her own. Long-suffering, self-denying, reflective, and intelligent, a constitutional reserve and taciturnity placed and kept her in the shade, and covered her mind, and especially her feelings, with a sort of nun-like veil, which was rarely lifted. Neither Emily nor Anne was learned; they had no thought of filling their pitchers at the well-spring of other minds; they always wrote from the impulses of nature, the dictates of intuition, and from such stores of observation as their limited experience had enabled them to amass. I may sum up all by saying, that for strangers they were nothing; but for those who had known them all their lives in the intimacy of close relationship, they were genuinely good and truly great."[17]

The message of Christianity ran through the novel *Agnes Grey* capturing Anne's own devout feelings where she taught her pupils to, "make Virtue practicable, Instruction desirable, and Religion lovely and comprehensible"[18] Indeed, she stated that "the best way to enjoy yourself is to do what is right and hate nobody. The end of Religion is not to teach us how to die, but how to live; and the earlier you become wise and good, the more of happiness you secure"[19]

In her novel *Agnes Grey*, Anne Bronte used her own experiences as a governess and did not shy away from the realistic fortunes of a young teacher. Agnes Grey demonstrated an outstanding patience as a governess. In complete contrast to *Wuthering Heights,* this novel held none of the Gothic features, with the exception of the small monsters who were to be educated, added to the ritual humiliations of the governess. The novel was very well told, highlighting the morals, or lack of them, of middle-class society, their social lives and relationships.

Anne 's second novel *The Tenant of Wildfell Hall* provided a psychological and sociological view of courtship, marriage and domestic abuse. Those themes were a brave departure from her previous novel, being controversial for the time in which they were written, revolving around the portrait of a captive wife married to a cruel and evil man, her escape and subsequent relationships with those around her. Anne Bronte, in her *Preface* to *Tenant* claimed she "may have gone too far" in the depiction of her characters, but maintained "it is better to depict them as they really are than as they would wish to appear."[20]

The novel had a serious message aimed at young ladies to avoid the trap of 'falling into the very error of my heroine.' Anne Bronte claimed that cruel and heartless men were common in society and that her novel was to expose such vices and issue a warning against them. As she stated, marriage was an important social event in the Victorian life of a young woman; they were brought up with the expectation of being a wife and mother. The mating game put a lot of pressure on the female, who would often have to marry to suit their family's needs rather than their own there were few alternatives for women during the nineteenth century. Also, there were fewer men than women, meaning that men could pick and choose; beauty and accomplishments were considered highly desirable. If a man was rich and handsome, he was much coveted. But, Anne Bronte warned against being persuaded by good looks without knowing the true character of the person you are to marry. However, the differences between the numbers of female and male marriageable adults often meant younger girls would marry older men, or, men who, as in the novel, wanted both a compliant, submissive wife, whilst continuing to live freely themselves.

Anne would have been witness to her brother's decline into alcoholism, which would have given her the evidence to describe its terrible effects on her character Huntingdon, and how family were also affected. In the novel Helen found her own relationship with others became difficult, and protecting her child became the most important issue. The escape scenes were significant and wove tension into the story of 'will she succeed?' the character of Helen was psychologically strong. We observed her feelings about the people around her, and her descriptions of nature and weather which echoed the current passions, similar to those employed by Emily. The twist in the tale, unexpectedly, was Helen's return to her husband, but on her terms, taking the advantage of drawing up a contract which she made him sign. His death throes were not glossed over by the author, but presented realistically, again, a sign that Anne must have witnessed Branwell's suffering as he died from alcoholic poisoning in his final days. She had always felt a sense of responsibility towards Branwell, having helped him to gain a position in the household in which she was teaching, but the affair with the wife of his employer, and her rejection of Branwell, led to his subsequent breakdown.

In the *Preface* of Anne's shocking novel she admitted, "I wish to tell the truth, for truth always conveys its own moral to those who are able to receive it...let it not be imagined, however, that I consider myself competent to reform the errors and abuses of society, but only that I would fain contribute my humble quota towards so good an aim, and if I can gain the public ear at all, I would rather whisper a few wholesome truths therein than much soft nonsense."[21]

Anne's unexpected death in 1849 brought an end to her novel writing, but had she lived, she would have become a writer of repute with her honest and straightforward observations of human nature.

Branwell Bronte, the only brother of Charlotte, Emily and Anne, was often depicted unkindly because of his dual personality. His early life had shown promise; involving himself in the literary and imaginative adventures of his sisters and the Gondal project. As he matured he endeavoured to find his way in the world but his inner insecurities led him into depression, pessimism and eventual dependence upon alcohol and opium. He had, however, along with his sisters, been a keen writer, and it was through his writing that he found an outlet for his emotions, ideas and thoughts.

According to Bettina L. Knapp, Branwell "wrote more than thirty volumes of stories, poems, plays, journals, histories, literary criticism, 'not counting those that have been lost or destroyed'[22] Music, which was important to Emily had also influenced Branwell, and he began flute and organ lessons, and travelled to see "orchestral performances of oratorios by Handel and Masses by Haydn and Mozart," returning home he wrote about music, interspersing such sequences amid depictions of war, banquets, theatrical productions, and other thrilling happenings, as evident in his six-volume *Letters to an Englishman* (1831)[23]

Branwell's last work, *And the Weary Are at Rest* (1845) was never completed, His last poem *Peaceful Death and Painful Life* was an appeal to God, and summed up his existence,

Why dost thou sorrow for the happy dead

For if their life be lost, their toils are o'er

And woe and want shall trouble them no more,

Nor even slept they in an earthly bed

So sound as now they sleep whilst dreamless, laid

In the dark chambers of that unknown shore

Where Night and Silence seal each guarded door:

So turn from such as these thy drooping head

And mourn the 'dead alive – whose spirit flies –

Whose life departs before his death has come –

Who finds no Heaven beyond Life's gloomy skies,

Who sees no Hope to brighten up that gloom;

Tis He who feels the worm that never dies –

The Real death and darkness of the tomb. [24]

Romer Wilson concluded that "all four Bronte children who survived to maturity were neurotic. Ann suffered from melancholia (religious variety). Charlotte at one time had an aggravated form of religious mania in which she nearly became insane through conviction of her own damnation...Branwell suffered from genuine delusions...Emily had what I believe is called persecution mania. Sense of inferiority, abnormal conceit gone the other way about, afflicted both Charlotte and Emily. In a sense Branwell and Emily were very mad and Charlotte intermittently mad. There is evidence that Charlotte was sick and went off her food, Emily wept or turned deathly pale and stark with temper, Ann groused, and Branwell drank, all to relieve their feelings in those circumstances which, tradition says, Mr. relieved his by pistol shooting."[25] Mrs Gaskell recorded how Charlotte had confided in her about Emily's temper, "when Emily's face whitened and her mouth set, when her eyes glowed in her pale face, and she compressed her lips to stone, no one dared to interfere with her."[26]

The three sisters had previously published their poems together in an anthology called *Poems by Currer, Ellis and Acton Bell* (1846). Emily produced many poems but just one novel, with its timeless quality; *Wuthering Heights* (1847) which has retained its popularity, being re-published and made into various film versions over the years.

A wider literary background which flourished in England during those early decades of the nineteenth century, and which were also strongly influenced by the Gothic/Romantic movement included Ann Radcliffe (1764-1823), following in the footsteps of Horace Walpole and his novel *The Castle of Otranto* (1764). Ann Radcliffe was the author of *A Sicilian Romance* (1797), *Gaston de Blondeville* (1(1790), *Romance of the Forest* (1791), *Mysteries of Udolpho* (1794) and *The Italian* (1826). Ann Radcliffe had also visited Germany with a group of friends, which she recorded in her book, *A Journey Made in the Summer of 1794 through Holland and the West Frontier of Germany* (1795). On arrival in the country she had a lot to say about the hospitality of the Germans, "the English habit of considering, towards the end of the day's journey, that you are not fat from the cheerful reception, the ready attendance, and the conveniences of a substantial inn, will soon be lost in Germany…whether you shall find a room, not absolutely disgusting, or a house with any eatable provision, or a landlady who will give it you, before the delay and the fatigue of a hundred requests have rendered you almost incapable of receiving it."[27]

Descriptions about the state of German houses recorded squalidness and decay, but a six day stay in Frankfurt revealed a more civilised way of life, containing a theatre which was "larger than the little theatre in the Haymarket, and in form, resembled that of Covent Garden…the boxes are let by the year …the performances are plays and operas alternately; both in German; and the music of the latter chiefly by German composers…the orchestra, when we heard it, accorded with the fame of German musicians, for spirit and precision."[28] Ann Radcliffe concluded that no other entertainment was required as people visited each other and entertained in their homes.

At the city of Worms, Ann Radcliffe and her friends saw at first hand the perils of war, as wounded soldiers arrived by the wagon load for treatment. The scene was later captured in *Mysteries of Udolpho*. In Worms, religion was the overriding element, as Dominican, Carmelites, Capuchins and Augustans, were said to have their own monasteries at Worms, with a convent for Cistercian and Augustine nuns, and a synagogue for the Jews. Convents and castles held a fascination for Ann Radcliffe, who catalogued all the details for use in her future novels.

The group passed on from Worms and the images which had affected them, through many villages until they came to Malta, where people referred to the old castle of Maltenberg as the Devil's Castle. Its powerful presence was to felt later in the Gothic novel *Mysteries of Udolpho,* by Ann Radcliffe, when she returned to England. Her novels included *The Mysteries of Udolpho*, (1794), *The Italian*, (1797), *A Sicilian Romance* (1809), and others. She was recognised for her prolific use of Gothic features which were very comprehensive in *Udolpho.* The heroine, Emily was faced with the evil Montoni in a mountainous castle, cold and menacing, with the threat of death always hanging in the air.

Within the picturesque scenes painted by Anne Radcliffe the novel appears at first to be totally engulfed within the confines of Romanticism, but on closer inspection she also noted the harsh realities; in *Udolpho* the wounded soldiers from the recent war, the poorer characters starving, enemies in the background, the threat of violence hanging over the mountains, hills, towns and villages. Those images existed as a reminder of the political and cultural climate existing in France, where royalty, nobility and the church still maintained their hold on the population. Coleridge commented that the *Mysteries of Udolpho* was "the most interesting novel in the English language."[29] Jane Austen, in her novel, *Northanger Abbey* also makes reference to *Udolpho*, with her heroine, Catherine Morland, "avidly reading it." [30] Matthew Gregory Lewis followed on from the success of Walpole with his novel *The Monk* (1796). The setting for the novel was in a Capuchin monastery in Madrid. The themes of the novel included deviousness, sexual abuse, murder, religion, temptation and the Devil.

Lewis took up the argument about celibacy, blaming it, and the confines of monastic life, for its rigid and controlling methods. He illustrated it through his character, Ambrosio, who fell for the temptations of the flesh, despite his previously untarnished reputation, and the Mother Superior who displayed no mercy or compassion, only coldness and cruelty to her nuns.

Ambosio's fall from grace led him to other temptations, and greater danger for the people with whom he came into contact, particularly the young woman,

Antonia, who suffered under his advances, and was ultimately murdered. Lewis did not stop at attacking monks, but his parallel plot, involving nuns was a further attack upon the Catholic Church. His message was quite effective; the cloth does not change the person underneath. *The Monk* was terrifyingly powerful novel, which followed in the footsteps of Ann Radcliffe's Udolpho. Lewis commented that he considered Udolpho to be "one of the most interesting books ever to be published."[31] Although *The Monk* had similar traits as Udolpho, it was a more shocking and terrifying novel. In the novels of Radcliffe we are shocked, but there are always simple explanations for uncanny events. With Lewis, there are the facts; terrifying, shocking and realistic, with no attempt to placate the reader. He makes the reader face evil and the Devil, with ghosts, skeletons, and black magic. Everything is there; a true Miltonic battle of good versus evil. Lewis made references in his novel to Germany and that his character, Alphonso," spoke German tolerably well,"[32] [and] "sang as loud as [he] could a little German air well known to her..."[33] Germany was popular in England at the time the book was being written, and many novels made reference to it, as it was one of the main influences on literature during that period. Thomas love Peacock, in his novel, *Nightmare Abbey* (1818), had commented that his main character Scythrop could be observed with a copy of "*The Sorrows of Werther* in his hand...He began to devour romances and German tragedies, and by the recommendation of Mr. Flosky, to pour over ponderous tomes of transcendental philosophy, which reconciled him to the labour of studying them by their mystical jargon and necromantic imagery."[34]

The Gothic romance of *Udolpho* and the supernatural Gothic of Lewis was followed by another form of the Gothic; the scientific. Mary Shelley (1797-1851), was a prolific writer of the period. Her most famous novel, *Frankenstein*, explored the dangers of the romantic with the scientific thinker's imagination, leading to a horrifying creation. By attempting to play God and continue with an over zealous attempt to create a man-made 'human,' the consequences of such an experiment were never taken into account. The scientist, Frankenstein, who had always been curious about natural sciences and the occult, became as monstrous as his creation when he promised to make a mate for the monster and then realising that he was perpetuating the situation he had created, he destroyed it.

The story revealed the shocking truth of innocence lost, despair and the seeking of revenge. Who could have predicted, through the horror of such a grotesque creature, there lurked an emotional being that learned about the joy of birth, reading books, education, and finally the human power of rejection and prejudice.

It proved to be an international best seller. Like Anne Radcliffe, Mary Shelley employed the use of Gothic and Romantic techniques and landscapes in her novels. The cold, bleak landscapes echoed the isolation of Frankenstein's monster, who was not recognised by the human beings surrounding him, or by nature itself.

Although recognised for her creation of the novel *Frankenstein*, Mary Shelley also produced novels called *The Last Man*, *Valperga* (*1821*) and *Matthilda* (*1819*), which were written after the turn of the century.

The themes of suffering, pain, guilt, anxiety and redemption were to be found in all Gothic literature of the nineteenth century, with the major novel of

Melmoth the Wanderer leading the way. Its author Charles Maturin (1782-1824), had been brought up in Dublin, where he spent his entire life working for the Church. He held a gift for writing, literature and drama, producing novels and plays which always contained the central character of Satan.

After some initial success with writing both novels and dramas, he was inspired, when giving a sermon one day, to write a novel which would make a strong impact upon the present reading public, but which would be remembered for years afterwards. *Melmoth* was an epic piece of literature, with typical Gothic and Romantic elements, having an atmosphere of mystery and suspense. The sermon had contained questions about immortality and the afterlife. The structure of the novel was constructed from the many stories about the central character of Melmoth, the wandering Jew, from his initial appearance in Ireland, and the continued account of his travels through Spain and India, and his haunting appearances in situations where people were desperate for escape. The closure was his return to Ireland and death, following a hundred and fifty years of wandering the earth trying to find victims to share his fate, and elicit his escape from damnation. All of whom he attempted to capture refused to relinquish their faith, confirmed by the words, "No one has ever exchanged destinies with *Melmoth the Wanderer*. I have traversed the world in the search, and no one to gain that world, would lose his own soul."[35]

The different periods of action took place in an untimely and dark menacing world, in a labyrinth of subterranean tunnels, cells and passageways. Melmoth's immortality came with the freedom to be anywhere in the world, but which was also a heavy burden. The powerful imagination of Maturin, concentrated in the novel on the extreme suffering and evil practices of the Catholic Church which were condemned strongly by Maturin, as his characters suffered at their hands through psychological brainwashing, torture and other cruel methods. The initial episode of Monçada incorporated a powerful emotional realism in which he claimed, "The truth may be horrible to the inmates of a convent, whose whole life is artificial and perverted."[36] Torture was a regular device employed in the novel, especially in the scenes of the Spanish Inquisition, which created a strong emotional reaction from his readers. Religion and immortality, with terror, salvation, redemption and belief in God were combined to create a story in which humanity itself was the catalyst for all suffering.

The literary influences on Maturin were Pope, Crabbe, and Scott, but "he had little admiration for Byron, and none for Coleridge or Wordsworth." It was at odds that he wrote such black and violent despair where logic and elegance had no place…His Melmoth, human but exempt from death, a lost soul and a tempter, is descended from Faust and Mephistopheles, from the Flying Dutchman and the Wandering Jew of European legends; Marlowe, Milton, Goethe, Godwin, Beckford, Schiller, Hoffmann, all contributed to the idea of this sardonic invulnerable rover with mesmeric eyes and a grating laugh."[37]

Nature had become a major theme of poets and writers, often within a religious context, such as in the works of Emily Bronte. Women had begun to compete with their male counterparts in this genre, although it had been established by poets such as Wordsworth and Coleridge. Both English and German Romantic poets, sought to express their feelings about, and within the natural world recording life as they perceived it.

Charlotte Smith (1749-1806) was both poet and novelist, her poems having that deep contemplative quality, similar to Emily 's later works, in which nature and the inner life became fused, where visions and atmospheres held the reader spellbound. The sonnet *To Melancholy (from the Elegiac Sonnets, 1784))*[38] was a good example of the Gothic/Romantic style with its eerie shadows and sounds. It was a very personal poem, set on the banks of the River Arun in October 1786, in which the poet described a stark, bleak, late evening landscape,'When latest autumn spreads her evening veil,' and where '...the grey mists from those dim waves arise.' There was no warmth in the poem, just a feeling of being accompanied by ghosts, or 'night-wanderers' from a previous time. It was a very visual poem, in which we see the scene as the poet did. It was one which would have delighted the Romantic artist to capture on canvas, as the mists rolled in from the river, with trees losing their foliage in a haunting atmosphere. Melancholy itself became personified and allowed the poet's closeness with nature to become almost mystic as she speaks of the 'visionary mind.'The conclusion was one of acceptance, as the memories, thoughts and feelings she had encountered brought a form of peaceful resignation rather than sadness.

'Oh Melancholy, such thy magic power

That to the soul these dreams are often sweet,

And soothe the pensive visionary mind![39]

Charlotte Smith was recognised for her continuing the themes of Romanticism and the Gothic but she had also held political views, and was a pioneer for women's causes, many of those issues surfaced in her novels. Death was a permanent feature in her novels, due to her own painful life from childhood. Like Emily Bronte, as a child, Charlotte Smith lost her mother, then later two of Charlotte's own children died. Because of her own painful life history those struggles were often incorporated into her works, which were many. She wrote twelve novels in total, from 1787 to 1798, with her final publication; *Letters of a Solitary Wanderer* in 1802, but because of her need to support herself and her children Charlotte Smith continued to write producing children's literature and non-fiction work such as two volumes about the *History of England* (1806) and *A Natural History of Birds* (1807).

Mary Robinson (1758-1800) had also been a respected poet and novelist during the Romantic years, alongside Anna Barbauld (1743-1825), Anna Seward (1742-1809), Hannah More (1745-1833), and Felicia Hemans (1793-1835) – but full and overflowing. Coleridge stated that "I never knew a human being with so full a mind – bad, good, and indifferent, I grant you." Her Romantic poem *The Haunted Beach* [40] encompassed all the ingredients of nature's expansive Romantic and Gothic landscape and seascape, with an influence from Coleridge's *Ancient Mariner*. Taken from her *Lyrical Ballads*, the poem comprises nine verses of nine line verse. It told the tale of shipwrecked mariners, and their ghosts who haunted the beach, 'Of spectres gliding hand in hand/ Where the green billows played/And pale their faces were as snow/and to the skies, with hollow eyes...The clear moon marked the ghastly crowd.' From the ghostly apparition the poet tells of the one who made it to the shore, only to be murdered for his plunder, although there is no direct evidence given by the poet, except to mention the Spanish gold under his arm. 'For in the fisherman's lone shed/A murdered man was laid/With ten wide gashes on his head/...About his arm he made/A packet rich of Spanish gold.' The probability was that any remaining gold would be lying at the bottom of the sea, taken down as the ship sank. The poem took a twist at the end, as the lonely fisherman watching the scene every night is identified as the murderer, whose guilt repeatedly brought him back to the scene, 'For thirty years his task has been/Day after day more weary;/For Heaven designed his guilty mind/Should feed on prospects dreary/Bound by a strong and mystical chain...He wastes, in solitude and pain/A loathsome life away.' Isolation, guilt, and nature itself took hold of his mind as he watched the ghostly images from the beach taunting him, trapping him in a dark reality. The poem, like that of Coleridge, had a mystical element, with its eerie sounds and sights, the gloomy atmosphere and isolation of the lone fisherman, and his ultimate divine retribution for the crime committed.

Women had made great advances in the field of literature, and popular poet and novelist Mary Robinson stated in *Blackwoods* (1824) 'The best novels that have been written, since those of Smollet, Richardson, and Fielding, have been produced by women: and their pages have not only been embellished with the interesting events of domestic life, portrayed with all the refinement of sentiment, but with forcible and eloquent, political, theological and philosophical reasoning. To the genius and labours of some enlightened British women posterity will also be indebted for the purest and best translations from the French and German languages...Poetry has unquestionably risen high in British literature from the productions of female pens; for many English women have produced such original and beautiful compositions, that the critics and scholars of the age have wondered, while they applauded.'[41] The time was ripe for the three Bronte sisters to enter, what had been for many years, a man's world.

CHAPTER TWO: Emily Bronte: Poems, Themes and Influences

The themes and poetic influences of Emily Bronte included those from Germany and the Gothic, Subjectivity and Imagination, alongside the natural world providing its eternal and mystical backdrop. Despite a lack of biographical data about Emily Bronte there has been renewed interest in her work in recent years. However, much of that interest has often been towards her novel *Wuthering Heights*, which also received critical attention for its Romantic-Gothic influence.

Many biographers and critics have endeavoured to deconstruct the poetry of Emily Bronte, to interpret its subsequent meanings. Trying to piece together a picture embracing her teachers, 'muses' and influences is not so easy. We have to look at the time in which she was writing in the early nineteenth-century, and at the type of literature she was reading. One constant source of inspiration was her beloved moors, where she could wander freely and contemplate nature in all its glory, away from the pressures of harshness and inequalities of life. Landscape was a major theme for the Romantic writer, poet, musician or artist, capturing its colourful beauty or its dark cruelty. Emily embraced both, capturing the different moods and scenes, feeling at one with Mother Nature and the infinity of the universe. The additional themes of the poetry were subjective and personal; freedom, isolation, death and dreams, whilst always in a religious context, questioning life after death, God and the meaning of life.

Despite the huge support for her father and his work in the church, Emily, as she grew up questioned her religious beliefs and the oppressive Protestant-Calvinist ravings about Heaven and Hell, but also about the position of the individual in that argument. Those Methodist sermons, according to Patricia Ingham, "made the assumption that each listener had a soul worth saving, whatever their social position or status. She continued, "Patrick Bronte belonged to this wing and he had evangelical patrons...His wife and her sister, Aunt (Elizabeth) Branwell, were both brought up as Methodists but joined the Anglican community, a choice made easier by Patrick's evangelicalism. So a felt individual faith was the model on which the Bronte children were brought up."[1] When reading the Bronte poems and novels their religious beliefs and attitudes can be easily detected.

Arthur Pollard claimed that the religious terminology of much of Emily 's poetry did not obscure the fact that hers was no conventional religion (despite her father's calling). "So far as her intensely personal beliefs can be defined, she was a Pantheist, seeing all Life as One –the Visible and the Invisible, the human, the elemental, the animal and vegetable all imbued with the same spiritual forces."[2]

According to A. Mary F. Robinson, however, "it was this very Calvinism [which] influenced her ideas, this doctrine she so passionately rejected, calling herself a disciple of the tolerant and thoughtful Frederick Maurice, and writing in defiance of its flames and shrieking, the most soothing consolations to mortality that I remember in our tongue."[3]

Frederick Maurice, saw how the nation was becoming divided by social and political unrest, and believed that "a national church was indispensable to the maintenance or restoration of national unity."[4] He introduced the Christian Socialist Movement and Working Men's College "in a bid to bring a form of social and spiritual democracy. His Christian Socialism was frequently misunderstood and led him into conflicts of opinion with his peers. He believed that a true socialism [was] the necessary result of a sound Christianity."[5] His sermon *The Kingdom of Christ* (1838) was just one of his progressive and forward-thinking pleas for religious unity. His *Theological Essays* (1853) brought his eventual dismissal from King's College.

The changing world of the nineteenth century had affected all walks of society, but the dominating questions of the day continued to revolve around religion. Having accepted previous forms of religious beliefs, people became open to new interpretations of Christianity. Emily Bronte was a private and solitary person but was brought up surrounded by her slightly dysfunctional family. She was also aware of the presence of God, being surrounded by the church and its teachings through her father, not to mention the ever-present graveyard. Having many sides to her personality, she had often been labelled as 'mystic.' In her poetry she talked about dead family members and friends around her, who remained as shadows on the earth and visited her at night.

The following essay (*devoir*) written originally in French, during her stay in Brussels, was inspired by the caterpillar and butterfly, allowing Emily to voice her innermost thoughts about God, nature and creation. I have included the full version for students who may not have had access to an English translation.

□ *The Butterfly (Le Papillon)*

In one of those moods that everyone falls into sometimes, when the world of imagination suffers a winter that blights its vegetation; when the light of life seems to go out and existence becomes a barren desert where we wander, exposed to all the tempests that blow under heaven, without hope of rest or shelter – in one of these black humours, I was walking one evening at the edge of a forest. It was summer; the sun was still shining high in the west and the air resounded with the songs of birds. All appeared happy, but for me it was only an appearance. I sat at the foot of an old oak, among whose branches the nightingale had just begun its vespers. "Poor fool," I said to myself, "is it to guide the bullet to your chest or the child to your brood that you sing so loud and clear? Silence that untimely tune, perch yourself on your nest; tomorrow, perhaps, it will be empty." But why address myself to you alone? All creation is equally mad. Behold those flies playing above the brook; the swallows and fish diminish their numbers every minute. These will become, in their turn, the prey of some tyrant of the air or water; and man for his amusement or his needs will kill their murderers. Nature is an inexplicable problem; it exists on a principle of destruction. Each being must be the tireless instrument of death to others, or itself must cease to live, yet nonetheless we celebrate the day of our birth, and we praise God for having entered such a world.

During my soliloquy I picked a flower at my side; it was fair and freshly opened, but an ugly caterpillar had hidden itself among the petals and already they were shrivelling and fading. "Sad image of the earth and its inhabitants!" I exclaimed. "This worm lives only to injure the plant that protects it. Why was it created and why was man created? He torments, he kills, he devours; he suffers, dies, is devoured – there you have his whole story. It is true that there is a heaven for the saint, but the saint leaves enough misery here below to sadden him even before the throne of God.

I threw the flower to earth. At that moment the universe appeared to me a vast machine constructed only to produce evil. I almost doubted the goodness of God, in not annihilating man on the day he first sinned. "The world should have been destroyed," I said, "crushed as I crush this reptile which has done nothing in its life but render all that it touches as disgusting as itself." I had scarcely removed my foot from the poor insect when, like a censoring angel sent from heaven, there came fluttering through the trees a butterfly with large wings of lustrous gold and purple. It shone but a moment before my eyes; then, rising among the leaves, it vanished into the height of the azure vault. I was mute, but an inner voice said to me, "Let not the creature judge his Creator; here is a symbol of the world to come. As the ugly caterpillar is the origin of the splendid butterfly, so this globe is the embryo of a new heaven and a new earth whose poorest beauty will infinitely exceed your moral imagination. And when you see the magnificent result of that which seems so base to you now, how you will scorn your blind presumption, in accusing Omniscience for not having made nature perish in her infancy. God is the God of justice and mercy; then surely every grief that he inflicts on his creatures, be they human or animal, rational or irrational, every suffering of our unhappy nature is only a seed of that divine harvest which will be gathered when, Sin having spent its last drop of venom, Death having launched its final shaft, both will perish on the pyre of a universe in flames and leave their ancient victims to an eternal empire of happiness and glory.[6]

Written during her time in Brussels (1842), where Catholicism was deeply embedded, Emily's unhappiness, being away from home and all that was familiar was perhaps the reason for her emotional thoughts, in which she became distracted by the caterpillar and butterfly. It gave a very personal insight into her thoughts which reflected those felt by many people at some point in their lives; particularly when faced with the death of loved ones, the destruction of wars, personal crisis, and natural disasters. The single fateful event facing her her, led her to question the destructive aspects of nature, and on a deeper level why God allowed such evil to exist in his world. In her tortured frame of mind she crushed the caterpillar under her foot, and at that moment, and as though her thoughts were heard, the arrival of the beautiful butterfly made her realise how its freedom had been created by its death; a form of immortality. Nature's cyclical actions became clear to see as life, death and rebirth were constantly revolving, and the major question about life after death, which had been troubling Emily seemed to be answered by the spiritual presence of the butterfly. The essay contained all the elements normally found in her poems; God, death, and life after death; in which nature was the medium. In her novel *Wuthering Heights* the same cyclical action played a central role, in which death and destruction wrought by its main characters of Heathcliff and Catherine, were finally replaced by a new cycle; the innocence and hope of Hareton and the second Catherine.

In addition to that essay, Emily wrote about the cat (*Le Chat,* 1842), which had quite a different approach to the butterfly essay, as it was quite volatile, and political. It was very clear that Emily liked cats, and she took issue to defend them with an unknown source, venting her anger at the cruelty inflicted upon animals by humans.

I can say with sincerity that I like cats; also I can give very good reasons why those who despise them are wrong. A cat is an animal who has more human feelings than almost any other being. We cannot sustain a comparison with the dog, it is infinitely too good; but the cat, although it differs in some physical points is extremely like us in disportion. A cat, in its own interest, sometimes hides its misanthropy under the guise of amiable gentleness; instead of tearing what it desires from its master's hand, it approaches with a caressing air, rubs its pretty little head against him, and advances a paw whose touch is soft as down. When it has gained its end, it resumes its character of Timon; and that artfulness in it is called hypocrisy. In ourselves, we give it another name; politeness, and he who did not use it to hide his real feelings would soon be driven from society. 'But,' says some delicate lady, who has murdered a half-dozen lapdogs through pure affection, 'the cat is such a cruel beast, he is not content to kill his prey, he torments it before its death; you cannot make that accusation against us.' More or less, Madam. Your husband, for example, likes hunting very much, but foxes being rare on his land, he would not have the means to pursue this amusement often, if he did not manage his supplies thus: once he has run an animal to its last breath, he snatches it from the jaws of the hounds and saves it to suffer the same infliction two or three more times, ending finally in death. You yourself avoid the bloody spectacle because it wounds your weak nerves. But I have seen you embrace your child it transports, when he came to show you a beautiful butterfly crushed between his cruel fingers; and at that moment, I really wanted to have a cat, with the tail of a half-devoured rat hanging from its mouth to present as the image, the true copying of your angel. You could not refuse to kiss him, and if he scratches you both in revenge, so much the better. Little boys are rather liable to acknowledge their friends' caresses in that way, and the resemblance would be more perfect. They know how to value our favours at their true price, because they guess the motives that prompt us to grant them, and if those motives might sometimes be good, undoubtedly they remember always that they owe all their misery and all their evil qualities to the great ancestor of humankind. For assuredly, the cat was not wicked in Paradise.[7]

The essay is passionate and intense, also very graphic, being loaded with images aimed to reinforce the message of how 'cruelty' is something that is 'learned.' The child is referred to as an 'angel,'but, like the cat, his behaviour is conditioned by those around him. Emily transferred the cruelty of animals to the cruelty of humans with her clear vision, placing those images into a religious speculation. The Bronte family had acquired many pets in the form of a dog named Keeper, a cat, "little black Tom, two tame geese called after the queen regent and the queen mother, 'Victoria' and 'Adelaide,' a hawk, Hero, which they had rescued from its abandoned nest up on the heights."[8] After drawing a picture of the hawk, Emily composed the following lines,

"And like myself lone, wholly lone,
It sees the day's long sunshine glow;
And like myself it makes its moan
In unexhausted woe.

Give we the hills our equal prayer;
Earth's breezy hills and heaven's blue sea;
We ask for nothing further here
But our own hearts and liberty.

Ah! could my hand unlock its chain,
How gladly would I watch it soar,
And ne'er regret and ne'er complain
To see its shining eyes no more.

But let me think that if to-day

It pines in cold captivity,

Tomorrow both shall soar away,

Eternally, entirely Free.[9]

Mrs Gaskell had written about the Bronte children's fondness of drawing

and painting, and how, "they would take and analyse any print or drawing which

came their way, and find out how much thought had gone to its composition, what

ideas it was intended to suggest, and what it *did* suggest. In the same spirit, they

laboured to design imaginations of their own; they lacked the power of execution, not

of conception..."[10] Mr. Bronte had employed "a teacher in drawing, who turned out to

be a man of considerable talent, but very little principle. Although they never attained

to anything like proficiency, they took great interest in acquiring this art; evidently,

from an instinctive desire to express their powerful imaginations.[11] Romanticism in

art had established itself during the nineteenth century through the works of Turner

and Blake in England, Friedrich in Germany, and Delacroix in France. Their

paintings embodied a spiritual vision of landscape and seascape, in which colour and

boundary were often blurred, giving an atmosphere of isolation, passion and

movement, defying and breaking down previous classical boundaries. Nature had

provided the Romantic artists with its awe-inspiring and jaw dropping vistas,

allowing them a freedom of the imagination which led to new heights of artistic

expression.

During her walks on the moors of Haworth, Emily would draw and write about the many species of wildlife, particularly the birds, including them in her journals. In her novel *Wuthering Heights,* the young Catherine had collected feathers from different varieties of birds and could identify them all, whilst in her poetry, Emily would wax lyrical about the ladybird, the linnet, the robin, insects and animals which she observed, writing, 'May flowers are opening/And leaves unfolding free/There are bees in every blossom/And birds on every tree.'(*May Flowers are Opening*)[12] and also,'Ladybird! Ladybird! Fly away home/Night is approaching, and sunset is come/The Herons are flown to their trees by the Hall/Felt, but unseen, the damp dewdrops fall/This is the close of a still summer day/Ladybird! Ladybird! Haste! fly away![13]

Bettina L. Knapp recalled how "Emily's intense love for everything that lived in nature kept her spirits and lust for life high, so that some came to call her a pagan." She continued,"Most especially she enjoyed the companionship of dogs. Hers, the large and fierce 'Keeper' from whom she demanded complete discipline, obeyed no one but Emily, yet had his moments of savagery. Like all pets, Keeper enjoyed jumping on the beds, but Emily's Aunt Branwell had forbidden it. When Emily discovered her dog on the bed she punished him by using "her bare fists to beat him." As Bettina Knapp pointed out, "Other incidents of this nature revealed Emily's capacity for both love and cruelty. When a strange dog bit her in the street she took a red-hot iron to cauterize the wound, preferring to keep the incident a secret from her family until the incubation period for rabies was over."[14]

Charlotte Bronte spoke of how quiet Emily had been in Brussels, but when the opportunity arose for her to be spontaneous in her writing, she poured her thoughts freely onto paper, with Charlotte accepting that Emily wrote the best devoirs (essays). Charlotte had also commented how Emily and Monsieur Heger "don't draw well together at all. Emily works like a horse, and she has had great difficulties to contend with, far greater than I have had."[15] She also added that "Emily would sit stiff and silent, unable to say a word, longing to be somewhere at her ease."[16] That place was home, which Emily longed for, with its familiarity, and where she could be herself.

From Mrs Gaskell we can put gather the jigsaw pieces that formed the life of Emily Bronte, and how nature had influenced her life. Mrs Gaskell stated that Emily's sister Charlotte had commented,

'My sister Emily loved the moors. Flowers brighter than the rose blossomed in the blackest heath for her – out of a sullen hollow in a livid hill-side, her mind could make an Eden. She found in the bleak solitude many and dear delights; and not the least and best loved was – liberty. Liberty was the breath of Emily's nostrils, without it she perished…her vision of home and the moors rushed on her, and "darkened and saddened the day that lay before her.'[17]

Clement Shorter gave an actual physical description of Emily having "a lithesome, graceful figure. She was the tallest person in the house, except her father. Her hair, which was naturally as beautiful as Charlotte's, was in the same unbecoming tight curl and frizz, and there was the same want of complexion. She had very beautiful eyes- kind, kindling, liquid eyes; but she did not often look at you as she was too reserved. Their colour might be said to be dark grey, at other times dark blue, they varied so. She talked very little. She and Anne were like twins – inseparable companions and in the very closest sympathy, which never had any interruption."[18]

A. Mary F. Robinson also commented upon Emily's appearance in the year 1833, when "she had grown into a tall, long-armed girl, full grown, elastic of tread, with a slight figure that looked queenly in her best dresses, but loose and boyish when she slouched over the moors, whistling to her dogs, and taking long strides over the rough earth. A tall, thin, loose-jointed girl–not ugly, but with irregular features and a pallid, thick complexion. Her dark brown hair was naturally beautiful, and in later days looked well, loosely fastened with a tall comb at the back of her head, but in 1833 she wore it in an unbecoming tight curl and frizz. She had very beautiful eyes of hazel colour...aquiline nose, a large expressive, prominent mouth. She talked little...she as a great walker, spending all her leisure on the moors...Never was a soul with a more passionate love of Mother Earth, of every weed and flower, of every bird, beast and insect that lived."[19]

When we examine the works of another writer or poet, we look with an objective eye at the quality of the work itself without reference to that author's life or background. The case of Emily Bronte, however, is unique, as she was one of three sisters from Yorkshire, all writing at the same time, as they had done from childhood. People were puzzled by the dialect used by Emily, as well as her Yorkshire characters and setting. No wonder the readers wanted to know more about that 'unique' woman and her sisters.

James Fotheringham stated that Emily's "Parentage and bias of nature, her life-long environment, and what we may term her vital education, go far to account for the woman and writer we know, and the elements and forces in them had a fuller and franker play right through her nature and her life that usually happens in the present century."[20]

The elements and forces of Emily's life would have indeed contributed to her poetic development, including her motherless upbringing, the Church, the moors and Yorkshire landscape, coupled with the desire to read and to learn, were all part of that 'life-long environment,' that would influence and nurture her enquiring mind, which fluctuated between romance and reality – the reality of her existence, and the romantic escape to her secret writing where her imagination would soar. Meditation and reflection on life and death was a powerful force for the German Romantic poets, and Emily Bronte, as they sought the world of eternity through their isolated positions. The German poets stressed the discontinuity of time in which there existed a spiritual presence. Irene Tayler stated that Emily came to her "reading of Romantic poetry with an already deep-rooted disposition to rebel against the limitations of life, against the authority not only of parent and teacher, but of all received opinion, a deep suspicion of all forms of power or thought whose source is not the self."[21] The essence of Romantic knowledge was the quest for eternity, coined by Novalis in the statement, "nothing is more attainable to the mind than infinity."[22]

Reading was Emily's pastime whether from her father's literary collection or magazines, such as *Blackwood's* and *Fraser's*, which formed a vital link with a wider and more intellectual world. According to Lucasta Miller, "unlike today's magazines, these periodical were not mere ephemera but would have been kept and re-read like books. They offered a mix of poetry, fiction, satire, criticism, philosophy, history and political commentary, often sustained to book-like length." On the subject of Romanticism she stated, "In the fallout from the Romantic Movement, these magazines fostered the belief that poets were not mere linguistic craftsmen, but privileged souls whose personalities were as important as their actual literary output."[23] *Blackwood's* magazine taught them that "literature was committed, not mere entertainment and frivolity," and that "works of the imagination were vehicles to convey a moral purpose."[24] Blackwood's also focussed heavily upon German literature which had been coming into the country, and would have provided much inspiration as well as entertainment. John Hewish suggested that Emily would have read the works of Hoffmann (a later influence for *Wuthering Heights*) and other German tales which were published in *Blackwood's*, including the works by Goethe.[25]

Mrs Gaskell stated that she had suspected the Bronte children had "no children's books, and that their eager young minds browsed undisturbed among the wholesome pasturage of English literature" and that "they took a vivid interest in the public characters and the local and foreign politics discussed in the newspapers."[26]

A visit to the Bronte Museum revealed a selection of the remaining books the family had held in their collection, and which would have been available for Emily to read. They included Edmund Burke's *Philosophical Enquiry into the Sublime and Beautiful* (a seminal work in Romantic aesthetics (London: J.F.Dover, 1827), John Milton's *Paradise Lost* (Edinburgh: J. Robinson and J. Gillies, 1792), Rabenhorst's *Pocket Dictionary of the German Language* (London: Longman, Brown and Company, 1843), *Deutches Lesebuch*, or, *Lessons in German Literature* (London: Duval and Company, 1837) The question arises, 'could it have been this book Emily was studying?' Mrs Gaskell had told us that "anyone passing by the kitchen door might have seen her studying German out of an open book."[27] Charlotte Bronte had also been learning German, and during her trip to Brussels, "a knowledge of German (now) became her object," and "she resolved to compel herself to remain in Brussels till that was gained."[28] Brussels had been the first experience of foreign travel by Charlotte and Emily, who "hated the country and people. They had been brought up as ultra-protestants. Their father was an Ulster man and his one venture into the polemics of his day was to attack the proposals for Catholic emancipation. With that inheritance of intolerance, how could Charlotte and Emily face with kindliness the Romanism which they saw around them?"[29]

Germany had remained popular in the Bronte collection, which contained *Schiller's Collected Works* (Ersterband: Stuttgart und Tubingen, 1838), demonstrating an interest in the German poet, which may have followed the series of articles on German literature, which were being published in England after 1820.

Added to this was Thomas Carlyle's *Life of Schiller*, which was being published serially in *The London Magazine* from 1823 to 1824, and then appeared in book form in 1825. The remaining books consisted of a variety of works by Sir Walter Scott, "who had also collected a number of German books – over three hundred volumes, including the works of Goethe, Schiller and the Schlegel brothers."[30] Scott was an enthusiastic student of German and had translated a number of texts. The themes of his own novels were "borrowed from German sources until near the end of his life, and he always acknowledged his indebtedness to German literature for situations and characters occurring in his writings."[31]

Other books remaining from the Bronte collection included a selection of Biblical and Devotional works, including Edward Young's *Night Thoughts on Life; Death and Immortality* (London: J F and C Rivington, 1790), which Emily had no doubt read many times. Nature played an important role for the Romantic writer, providing mood and atmosphere for the subjective vision of the poet, often as an accompaniment and animated object.

It was through nature that the poet could question and seek answers about God, man and creation. One of the favourites to emerge from the collection was *The Poems of Ossian* by James Macpherson, which had been annotated throughout by Charlotte, Emily, Anne and Branwell, indicating their fondness for the Gaelic poet. Ossian's tales of traditional hero figures may have been a large influence for the Gondal and Angrian tales invented by the Bronte children. John Hewish suggested that "Gondal may have been an Ossianic version of the local name – another link with with the common stuff of European Romanticism…the tone and ideology reflecting the legacy of Romantic literature, modified by Emily's own outlook."[32] Ossian's poems of supernaturalism and melancholy were very popular on account of translations by James Macpherson (although there were many fabrications and translations of the poems), and their fame spread across the continent to Germany where they were much appreciated by the German Romantic poets, including Goethe and Schiller. The appeal of the poems lay in qualities such as primitivism and the sublime, "grand, pathetic, serious, grave, wild and romantic, sublime and tender," were some of the epithets used to describe Ossian's *Fingal*.[33] The myths contained qualities that were readily available to the Romantic poets. Myths had always held a timeless appeal, because despite being fictitious they illustrated universal truths. The mystery of nature, a subject close to the heart of Romanticism, had always been explored through mythology, being explained as the will and action of the gods. The forces of nature were symbolised by gods of the sky, land and sea, embracing the nature spirits of the forests, fields and rivers, who could create a storm or bring calm in vivid and powerful lyrical descriptions.

The various descriptions of Emily Bronte suggested a kind of mysticism, which some critics referred to as supernaturalism, or the Gothic element. Charlotte Bronte also employed such features in her novel Jane Eyre – the mad woman in the attic and the Gothic hero figure of Rochester. According to Mrs Gakell, Charlotte had been surprised when,

"One day in the autumn of 1845, I accidentally lighted on an ms volume of verses in my sister Emily's handwriting. Of course, I was not surprised that she could and did write verse. I looked it over, and something more than surprise seized me – a deep conviction that these were not common effusions, nor at all like the poetry women generally write. I thought them condensed and terse, vigorous and genuine. To my ear they had a peculiar music, wild, melancholy and elevating."[34] The astute comments made by Charlotte Bronte confirmed the spiritual and mystical qualities of Emily's poetry; its striking language, supernatural and Gothic effects, echoing the influence of the German Romantic poets. An example could be seen in Emily's poem A.G.A (1837), where, "There shines the moon, at noon of night…Looking down on the lonely moor."[35]

The images captured were of a wild landscape, an isolated scene in which the night and the moon became symbols of the spiritual world. The moors of Haworth, Emily's own cultural environment, coupled with the machinery of Romanticism, provided the setting for such supernatural Gothic scenes.

Mrs Gaskell also, gave a description of Haworth in very Gothic terms, using words such as 'bleak,' solitude,' and 'oppressive.'[36] As with all Romantic poets Emily enjoyed the isolation of the natural world in which to allow her mind to unfold and become nearer to the vision of eternity. The German poet Novalis commented upon 'self-alienation' as being "the source of all abasement, as well as…the ground of all true elevation. The first step will be insight into ourselves – detaching contemplation of ourself – to stop here would be to go only half-way. The second step must be the active glance outwards – the steady observation of the outside world."[37] The visionary ideology of the Romantic writer meant that he was always driven back into the workings of his own mind. The works of Emily Bronte are highly individual, and yet many traces of the Romantic Movement and its various strands, current in her day, may be found in them, such as the privacy of the individual and the workings of the human mind or consciousness.

The English Romantic writers and poets, Keats, Shelley, Byron (*Childe Harold*), Wordsworth and Coleridge brought inspiration with their freedom of expression, adoration of the beauty of nature and the emotional world of man, much in the same way as the German writers. Both Wordsworth and Coleridge explored the ideas of everything in nature being mystical, complex and having a life source. *Christabel* is one of the best of examples by Coleridge with its uses of Gothic language and features. Germany had held a huge influence over the thoughts of Coleridge, who "had visited Germany to attend lectures and read deeply in Kant, Schiller, Schelling, and A.W.Schlegel. These studies made him the most influential interpreter of German Romanticism and the foremost exponent of its organicist doctrines...His theory of the poetic imagination as a unifying and mediating power within divided modern cultures provided one of the central ideas of Romantic aesthetics."[38]

The world of poetry inhabited by Emily Bronte displayed many signs of a European influence with its distinguishing spirit and features of a deadly fatalism. Human existence, philosophically, artistically and geographically provided a context in which the quest for spiritual knowledge was sought, and she followed in the footsteps of the German Romantic poets to transcend the limits of human consciousness through her own private and personal vision. Mary Ward agreed, adding that,

"There can be no question that there were German Romantic influences…and among them were many kindling sparks from that unextinguished hearth of German poetry and fiction which played so large a part in English imagination during the first half of the century…In 1830 Carlyle reports triumphantly 'a rapid fervour for German literature'…during the time he was writing and translating for *The Edinburgh*, *The Foreign Review*, *Fraser's* and *Blackwood's*, also, through the years Charlotte and Emily … were delighting in it, one may find a constant series of translations from the Germans, or articles on German memoirs and German poets."[39] According to
Bayard Quincy Morgan,

"Carlyle was the greatest single interpreter of German literature…somehow or other, without having been in Germany, he had acquired a surprisingly accurate feel for even the subtlest aspects of German idiom and style…the beginning of a true appreciation of German literature in England might be dated from 1824, the year his *Life of Schiller*, and before Romanticism, with its German basis came to be understood as a belief that life could be lived by ideals rather than rules.
The literature and movement itself proved to be a turning point in the culture of Europe, where some of the greatest writers of the age were only partly committed to its ideals, but in such a way that their exact position within the romantic ideology

remains impossible to pin down. For these and other reasons, there can be no simple, pithy definition of the term Romanticism."[40]

Mark Kipperman stated that "the most Romantic poems begin with something very wrong," and that the poet has to "define his own predicament...overcoming his deepest anxiety...his weapons are few...and his magic in his faith in the human imagination."[41] That darker side of Romanticism became known as the 'Gothic' element, whereby writers and poets explored death, often in a nightmare setting.

The desolate landscape and atmosphere were all encapsulated into a world of shadows. *The Encarta World Dictionary* defined Gothic literature as being "characterised by gloom and darkness, often with a supernatural plot unfolding in an eerie or lonely location such as a ruined castle."[42] The major Gothic issues were itemised by Rictor Norton as being,

"The aesthetics of the sublime, religion and the supernatural; the influence of the ancient romance; the discourse of the Enlightenment; reason verses Romantic imagination – the hobgoblin machinery of vampires, spectres, orphans, the Inquisition, nuns, storms and ruined castles, labyrinths and mystic forests, alongside social themes of prison reform, revolutionary politics, mother-daughter relationships, illicit sexuality, sensibility and madness."[43]

It was the world of imagination which influenced Emily Bronte, from its early inception through the *Gondal* poems, to her later more philosophical approach. *Gondal* was the fantasy world the Bronte children had invented, splitting it into two domains, with *Angria* belonging to Charlotte and Branwell, and *Gondal* to Emily and Anne. There has been confusion surrounding the collection of poems as to whether they were all part of a *Gondal* sequence, or whether some pieces were written separately. "There have been a number of attempts at imaginative reconstruction ranging from American scholar Fanny E. Ratchford's account of *Gondal's Queen* (1955), to *Gondal,* a play by Martin Wade broadcast on Radio 4 in 1993."[44]

The *Everyman's Companion to the Brontes*[45] offers an extensive a-z glossary of *Gondal* characters and places, and if we were to put the poems back-to-back then some continuity would no doubt emerge, but, as Margaret Lane had pointed out, "*Gondal* is as tricky as a tidal marsh."[46] Both Angria and Gondal had a large cast of characters, but many of the Gondal texts, unfortunately, have not survived. From the pieces remaining we need to look to the poems for the narrative of events. Their titles have been a good indicator to their origins in Gondal. The major character in the Gondal sagas was the female A.G.A who appeared to seduce every man she came into contact with. Indeed, it was her lust for her companion's lover Amadeus, which was the catalyst for her further misguided adventures, such as her involvement with the guitar-playing Fernando de Samara. After the death of A.G.A came the male equivalent in the form of Julius Brenzaida, who, like Shakespeare's *Julius Caesar*, was stabbed whilst surrounded by people he thought he could trust.

The *Gondal* poems were written over many years, and had individual qualities that allowed content to be judged in isolation, especially for their Gothic/Romantic themes, where "nature was envisaged no longer as a passive object, but as an animate being, animals, trees, plants, even stones and stars are as much active inhabitants of the universe as man himself."[47] Having evolved over a number of years, *Gondal* had many themes, plots and settings, with its construction of imaginative kingdoms and rulers, following in the style of Ossian's myth-making. The German Romantic poets also produced many works containing mythological elements, "having their German origins in Northern Mythology, where, as late as 1600 a German writer would illustrate a thunder storm destroying a crop of corn by a picture of a dragon devouring the produce of the field with his flaming tongue and iron teeth."[48]

Goethe used the superstition of the elves in his poem *Erlkönig* (Elf King), which was based "on the belief that elves, who, as cloud or storm spirits, were feared because of their habit of stealing children and young men in order to increase their race."[49] Mythology for Emily Bronte emerged through her visionary moments in which "Earth's wilderness was round me spread [while] Heaven's tempests beat my naked head," from the Gondal poem written in the *Gaaldine Prison Caves to A.G.A* (1840),[50] to the spirit muse who is never very far away, "Spirits of Bliss, what brings thee here/Beneath these sullen skies?"[51]

The eternal wanderer, a feature of so many Romantic poems and texts, was the subject of *The Night-Wind* (1840) where the wind became the wanderer personified, "In summer's mellow midnight...The soft wind waved my hair...I needed not its breathing...But still it whispered lowly...And all their myriad voices/instinct with spirit seem...I said, 'Go, gentle singer/Thy wooing voice is kind/But do not think its music/Has power to reach my mind...would not leave me /its kiss grew warmer still."[52] She had previously called to the wanderer to "kneel thee down and pray,"[53] written in 1837.

W.H. Miller wrote about the *Gondal* poems, stating that the events depicted, "Did not become part of a vanished past after they had occurred. They functioned for Emily Bronte, just as religious myths functioned for the Greek poets and tragedians…In one sense the *Gondal* saga was a sequence of temporally related events, like history. In another sense it was the simultaneous existence of all its events in a perpetual present."[54]

The *Gondal* poems had a life of their own that Emily was reluctant to give up on. Her detachment from life and reality was of such severe severity that, even when she and Anne went on a journey to York, she had taken on her character's persona, "during our excursion we were Ronald Macalgin, Henry Angora, Juliet Angusteena, escaping from the palaces of instruction to join the royalists."[55]

The Gondal poem *A Sudden Chasm of Ghastly Light* (1837) was a powerfully imaginative poem, being a good example of the German Romantic style where nature can be seen at her most terrifying, with its "shrieking wind/smothering snow-clouds/chill chill whiteness," and in the landscape the Gothic elements emerged in "a ghastly light,"[with] "black ruins smouldering/plundered churches piled with dead/around the ruined hall," with "one black yew tree," which had "ghostly fingers." The images painted an "awful dream in which "the great Cathedral rose/most majestic."[56]

Those stereotypical Gothic scenes were part of the imaginative and colourful battle scenes of *Gondal*, with its mention of "Tyndrum's fall," and its "battle's madness." A closer reading of the poem revealed the landscape of death and destruction, with the past turning to the present and future as the poet rushes "down the dark oak staircase (of Haworth Parsonage?) To fling open the door and gaze up to the sky, "where every star/glowed like a dying memory," and where "the great Cathedral," was "Discrowned/On its own realm of buried woe."[57] It was a very powerful poem conveying many essential elements of Romanticism and the Gothic, whilst having its basis in *Gondal*. The content reflected the condition of man in the early nineteenth-century, representing that "dark passage between life and eternity," where the conscious and unconscious minds meet with a doppelgänger effect, an apparition (ghostly counterpart) in the form of a double or living person, or, a psychic projection caused by unresolved anxieties, inherited by the German Romantic Movement.

Many of the themes of Gothicism, such as the supernatural, nightmare landscapes, persecution and the uncanny, emerged from the German writers (the ancient Gothic language having its roots in one of the East Germanic groups of Indo-Europeans) which were adapted and employed in the Romantic Movement. Their influence upon Emily Bronte can be seen in many of her verses, especially the Gondal poems which explored death, exile and imprisonment. A good example can be found in the poem *The Prisoner* (1845) with its "dungeon-crypts…year after year in gloom and desolate despair…the vision is divine."[58] Imprisonment also led to questions about war and man's cruelty to man whilst professing belief and allegiance to God.

The poem contained the mystical experience; loss of consciousness and the descent of peace, bringing with it the divine vision. "Then dawns the Invisible; the Unseen its truths reveals."[59]

Other Gothic devices can be found in *The Philosopher* (1845), "A golden stream-and one like blood,"[60] and in *Honours Martyr* (1844), where "Bleak, bleak, the east wind sobs and sighs."[61] The poem *Death of A.G.A* was Emily's longest poem, composed between 1841 and 1844, it contains much Gothic machinery in the shape of "The blood streams down her brow/the blood streams through her coal-black hair."[62] Atmosphere created by darkness and gloom was a further Gothic example used by Emily Bronte as she described the moors and its many changing faces, "Still as she looked the iron clouds/would part and sunlight shone between/But drearily strange, pale and cold," compared with "A sudden chasm of ghastly light…And cold, how cold! Wan moonlight smiled."[63] Although it is difficult to find any one definition for Romanticism, the poems all have some identifying characteristics, such as "the powerlessness of reason and supremacy of fate, isolation and escape, the rebel, religious quests, mysticisms, beliefs, the natural and supernatural worlds [using] imagination as a retreat from a world [they] see as imperfect, unjust and unpoetic."[64]

The Visionary [65] poem had its analogue with *Hymns to the Night* [66] in that the poet described the silence and isolation of the poet who waited for his visitant to arrive, accepting transcendental power to be its guiding light. Both poets used the silence of the night in which to perceive the spirit world, and as Novalis had found initiation through love, Emily Bronte also claimed, "He for whom I wait…shall come like visitant of air." The poem was an acceptance of the power of the poet to wander the depths of his subconscious in order to discover the 'other' spirit world. For both poets the daytime brought a harsh reality, but the night brought peace and happiness as they could glimpse into the immortal realm.

This was confirmed in Emily 's poem *To Imagination*, where "So hopeless is the world without," but comfort came through "The world within [which] I doubly prize." Again she mentioned her visitor as "The hovering vision," [whose] "Benignant Power" brought "hope when hope despairs." The poem carried the shadow of death to which the poet is eager for, believing that there would be "A lovelier life from Death."[67]

Irene Tayler stated about Emily Bronte, "because of her mother's early death she found in the temporal world less of the divine presence that they (German Romantics) did, and thus found the argument for alienation and withdrawal, and eventually silence and even death itself, more compelling than it was for most of them."[68] We can find evidence that Emily mentioned her mother and death together in many of her poems. In the poem *At Castle Wood,* she stated "But I was bred the mate of care/the foster child of (sore) distress,"[69] and as though she had a premonition of her own early death, a fragment (1839) carried the following lines, "go to grave in youth's [first] woe/that doom was written long ago."[70]

The poems of Emily Bronte and Novalis were unique for their visionary qualities, but also because they were written at a time when Romanticism gave them the opportunity to develop their innate powers. It seems uncanny that both Novalis and Emily Bronte found longing for death to become an early reality, and for both it was a tragic destiny to their own mythical drama.

Despite the ironies of life's mirroring effect where "my spirit knew itself once more," the world for Emily Bronte provided her with poetic illusions that seeped into many of her poems, "Deepdown in the silent grave/With none to mourne above," was contrasted with "I am not and none beside," with its contrary mood.[71]

Barbara and Gareth Lloyd Evans commented that for Emily "the writing of poetry seems to have been much closer to a necessary act…found it the only way of communicating with or attempting to body forth a world elsewhere. And for all the technical resources at her disposal, the intensity of her need to remain in touch with that world makes her artlessness into a virtue."[72] Whether her art was a virtue or not, it would appear to have been a type of dependency, and in that respect a personal religion to which (like Novalis before her, whose spiritual inspiration changed him completely), she devoted her life.

Lilian Furst stated that "the Romantics poeticized reality, transforming it through the imagination, remaking the world according to a personal vision."[73] They tried a wide variety of verse forms, but whatever the differences, the similarities predominated; the result being an intensity of the imaginative vision, in which God, man, nature, finite and infinite, objectivity and subjectivity were interfused. Their revolutionary words reflected human thought in opposition to any rational or conventional methods, and they embraced the world of the imagination, which was to capture and retain the elements of nineteenth-century literature.

Stevie Davies described the doppelgänger as an "identity of opposites, so powerfully explored in German Romantic philosophy, [which] fascinated Emily Bronte, and made her reading of her own conflict into an analysis of universal significance and application. She wrote for a world of twoness in which each person, a near symmetrical figure, with two hands, eyes, ears and twin hemispheres of brain, is more often than not in 'two minds' talking to oneself, experiencing splits and divisions. Such divisions into left and right, yes and no, conscious and unconscious, at once threaten, and generate the energy which powers creativity."[74]

Lilian Furst stated that nature was the area in which Romantic poetry had "achieved its greatest fame," and that "the notion of Romantic poetry [was] for many people virtually synonymous with nature poetry."[75] The Romantic poets, however, differed widely in their attitudes towards nature, although shared a similar approach to it. Lilian Furst commented that it was the "fusion of man and nature, the mirror effect of nature being in sympathy with the poet, sharing his joys, and more often than not, his sorrows, that became the recognised feature of Romantic poetry."[76] Rupert Christian pointed out that "the Romantic simply conjured up in an endless series of mirrors magical visions without forms or limits of convention…space and time contract and dissolve; characters assume supernatural powers; plots are inconsequential and liable to change direction drastically."[77]

The Lakeland Poets, as they had become known, left a lasting legacy of literary works. Romantic literature in England found expression through the works of its poets Although Wordsworth and Coleridge were the first wave Romantic poets, they were followed by Keats, Byron and Shelley as the second wave. Ironically, Keats, Shelley and Byron all died abroad in Europe, Keats and Shelley in Italy and Byron in Greece, with just Wordsworth and Coleridge left to depart life in England.

Because of the unique range of styles and the time they were written, Lilian Furst[78] suggested that the poets be divided into rough categories, first proposed by Charles Hereford. The first 'division' was the Wordsworth group (1798-1806); Coleridge, Stowey, Crabbe and Clare, followed by Walter Scott's group of Campbell, Moore and Southey. Following on later were Shelley, Byron, and Keats (1818-1822).

Of the English Romantic poets Coleridge (1772-1834) was the most radical. He openly debated European religious anxiety, many of his sentiments being through such poems as *France; an Ode* (1798) and *Destruction of the Bastille*. The impressions of the French Revolution had left a deep mark leading to a nervous life-long affliction.

Coleridge produced his main visionary works such as *Kubla Khan, The Rhyme of the Ancient Mariner* and *Christabel*. The Gothic-supernatural aspect to a number of his poems contained all the hallmarks of German Romantic culture, with its dream-like and spiritual landscape of man within nature. By 1817, having matured in his outlook and thoughts, he became more involved with philosophy. He produced and attempted to define the terms of *Imagination and Fancy*, in which he discussed the activity of the creative mind with emphasis upon the poet and nature, concluding that through the selection of language there existed a type of freedom, "the primary imagination I hold to be the living power and prime agent of all human perception, and as a repetition in the finite mind of the eternal acts of creation in the infinite I AM…Fancy is indeed no other than a mode of memory emancipated from the order of time and space…which we express by the word choice. But equally with the ordinary memory, it must receive all its materials ready-made from the law of association."[79]

His investigation of the internal processes suggested the association of ideas which further suggested that Nature was created and controlled by God, as the "centre of energy."[80] Renwick suggested that the centre of energy could be seen in the images and visions of the Ancient Mariner, which made it a 'miraculous' poem. Charles Lamb too had said of the *Ancient Mariner* and its composition which played tricks with the mind, "I should like to see more of the tricks they played with Coleridge's mind, which is more interesting than mine."[81] Coleridge had, however, been taking opium at regular intervals, which may have influenced his dreamy, vision-like qualities, helping to produce supernatural and romantic visions.

Coleridge spent ten months in Germany, where his ideas took a different path in philosophy, following time spent at the University of Göttingen. There he studied Germanic philology, physiology, and theology, and also planned to write a book about Lessing. His Christian beliefs were echoed when he wrote, "That God is everywhere! The God who framed/Mankind to be one happy family/Himself our Father, and the World our Home."[82] His later poems included *Religious Musings* and *Destiny of Nations*.

The *Biographia Literaria* (1817), was one of the most memorable and analytical documents produced by Coleridge. According to Rupert Christiansen, it was "a book, like Coleridge's life, of grand intentions and broken promises, diving into digressions, ambling into anecdotes, and plastering up the cracks with chunks of impenetrable philosophy secretly lifted straight from the writings of the German philosopher Schelling."[83] He suggested, perhaps sarcastically, that it was an experiment in the freedom of the mind, the theory that Coleridge had earlier established. The book had set out to define the nature of poetry, and the nature of the poet and his psychological make-up or creative imagination. It pointed to the poet as a medium for the soul of all mankind, and so in some ways having the ability to transform the world. Coleridge claimed that the poet's imagination was part of nature and so a natural power, and it was with those sentiments that Christiansen concluded, "Coleridge's thinking has one shining virtue; it responds intimately to personal feeling and experience, taking us closer to him than we can come to perhaps in any of his contemporaries."[84] The creative freedoms and theories of the artists all sprang from the influence of Germany, with its Enlightenment and following Romantic writers and philosophers.

Wordsworth was another of the Lake poets to be admired by writer and poet, De Quincey – the two had later been friends for about twenty years, during De Quincey's time in the Lake District. The biography has been changed and added to over the years to give an even fuller account of influences in each part of De Quincey's life. The remainder of his life was spent putting together a collection of essays. During his lifetime De Quincey had been a 'prolific essayist and his eventual collection amounted to approximately sixteen volumes,' according to George Saintsbury.[85]

Lord David Cecil in *The English Poets*, offered a condensed appraisal of well-known poets through the ages, and referred to English poetry as being ideally suited for description, or for the expression of emotion, "as its very richness helps it to evoke those indefinite moods, those visionary flights of fancy of which so much of the material of poetry is composed. There is no better language in the world for touching the heart and setting the imagination aflame."[86]

Lord Cecil spoke of Wordsworth (1770-1850), as being "the first great poet of the [Romantic] period, [being] a mystic of nature." He continued, "now and then inspiration seizes him; and he rises to a height of serene, spiritual sublimity unparalleled in English poetry," and that "unlike Blake he is never so rapt into the world of his vision as to lose sight of the common earth."[87]

According to Paul Hamilton, "it is Wordsworth and Byron, not Coleridge and Shelley, who have remained the touchstones of canonical English poetry of the romantic age. In Wordsworth and Byron inhere the definite contrasts of the period's sensibility and style, the consistent Englishness of the former and the cosmopolitan inconsistency of the latter."[88] He pointed out that although the poetry of Wordsworth, with its major themes of the natural world and man's place in it, has been widely popular since his death, whilst Wordsworth was alive he was writing with some degree of anonymity. One special friendship was forged with Samuel Taylor

Coleridge.

Lord Cecil's comments invited a comparison with the poems of Goethe, Novalis and the other Romantic poets as he called Wordsworth, "the supreme poet of spiritual existence who can both convey those moments of celestial glory, in which man penetrates beyond the veil of the flesh, and also show them in their true relation to the confined prosaic round of every day existence."[89] The works of Wordsworth were many, but his recognisable ones came in the form of *The Prelude* and *Lyrical Ballads*, the scenes of which reflected the subjective actions and feelings of the poet, as well as the narrative aspect recalling Wordsworth's early life in which he meditated upon events for their significance. The poetry of Wordsworth was centred in nature and its spiritual aspects, an affinity he shared with his German counterpart, Jean Paul. Both conveyed the wonderful and sublime natural aspects of sunsets, stars, the changing skies, seas and oceans.

Wordsworth's friendship with Coleridge, stated Rupert Christiansen, brought new visions as "both men were profoundly united in the belief that the world and everything in it down to the barest motionless existence of rocks and stones – was alive and interrelated, that there was something one and indivisible beneath all the surface diversity of appearance."[90]

For Emily Bronte, nature represented much more than its physical appearance. The moorland landscape became infuse with every sound and every colour that could transform it into a visionary and haunting place, where she found through her heightened sensibilities, a sense of liberty in her contemplation of, and desire for death. Charles Simpson, discussing the Yorkshire moors, stated how

"Storms gather swiftly on these hills. They seem to emanate from the very earth. The low moaning of the wind bearing the scud of rain rises out of a central darkness, brooding, ponderous, livid, as only clouds bearing down over a landscape so sullen can be. They come with shades of night in the hollows. They echo with tones of thunder unheard in the sheltered valleys below. The acoustic properties of the moor yield strange voices. Echoes hold variants of the storm-notes, carried from one ridge to another. Sounds gain emphasis from repetition in different keys as though each hillside took up its own response, swelling the gamut of agitation and discord with a voice peculiar to its reception."[91]

The poem *Loud without the wind was Roaring* (1838) explored the moorland setting in all its guises, calling them "my dear moorlands," which dance between the seasons echoing an "ancient song." The wind became a companion "in its glory and pride," speaking to the poet, calling "from valleys and highlands," whilst the cornfields were "all waving," and "the bright sun was beaming." The poem suggested that Emily was thinking about her home, and how the wind would sound so loud on the exposed northern moors. away from her familiar surroundings when the poem was written. Her sadness at being away from the moors was confirmed in the lines, "the grim walls enfold me/I have bloomed in my last summer's sun," and how "The spirit that bent'neath its power...burned to be free." The landscape and the poet shared spiritual bond; "A deep fountain who's springing/Nor Absence nor Distance can quell." The poem ended on a hopeful note of longing to return to the moors where "the loved and the loving/shall meet on the mountains again."[92]

According to Ellen Nussey, the moors had been an inspiration to Emily from an early age when "in fine and suitable weather delightful rambles were made over the moors [where] every moss, every flower, every tint and form were noted and enjoyed. Emily especially had a gleesome delight in these nooks of beauty – her reserve for a time vanished. One long ramble made in these early days was far away over the moors to a spot familiar to Emily and Anne which they called 'The Meeting of the Waters.' It was a small oasis of emerald green turf, broken here and there by small clear springs; a few large stones served as resting places; seated here we were hidden from all the world, nothing appearing in view but miles and miles of heather, a glorious blue sky, and brightening sun."[93]

The poem *Often Rebuked Yet Always Back Returning* (undated) looked back to the early days and "those first feelings that were born with me," where Emily could escape the real world which "was too strangely near," in favour of freedom and the moors, "where the grey flocks in ferny glens are feeding/Where the wild wind blows on the mountain side." Freedom was a necessary act of survival where the poet affirmed she would "walk where my own nature would be leading/It vexes me to choose another guide."[94] Solitariness provided a canvas for her imagination where she could be at one with nature. The poem was quite philosophical and without illusion as it questioned "What have those lonely mountains worth revealing?" Her own logic offered the answer "More glory and more grief than I can tell." Nature is ever-present and sees all; it is the world of "Heaven and Hell," bringing happiness as well as sadness; the seasons ever-revolving, like the evolution of man. Although a reflective poem, it did contain many Romantic emotive phrases that recalled Emily's ability to transcend reality, as "visions rising, legion after legion," and "the earth that [can] wake *one* human heart to feeling, with its stress on the word 'one' finally achieving a reconciliation with cyclical nature through the vision of entering eternity.

Sir Herbert Read concluded that "there is about the moors of Yorkshire, where they yet remain, a quality that works on the mobile senses. Their sparseness and loneliness drives you to an intimacy with whatever life does exist there; a small thing like the scent of a bog myrtle can kindle a strong emotion…the human mind is perhaps heard more distinctly in this inorganic stillness…when it has learned to think, and to express its thoughts. The moors are merely material for observation and perception, and if, into their confines there happens to enter a mind of exceptional dimensions, this mind will use its environment to some purpose. Such was the case with Emily – placing her firmly within the Romantic Movement."[95]

The revolutionary aspect of Emily 's Romanticism, like that of the German poets, resulted in an alienation from society or even from nature itself, which could be represented as a hostile, as well as comforting source. The poem *The Night is Darkening Around Me* (1837) [96] had an oppressive Gothic atmosphere, where nature would cast its powerful spell with "wild winds" that "coldly blow," trees are bending" eerily as their "boughs 'Gothic' representation with the poet being helpless, unable to move, a landscape with clouds gathering thickly overhead, giving the vision of a wasteland. The poem was a disturbing fragment indicating the poet's loss of faith and inspiration, being isolated in a cold forbidding environment. Many of the fragment poems had a 'Gothic' feel to them, including *Lonely at her Window Sitting* (1838)[96] where the "fitful winds foreboding flitting/Through a sky of cloudy grey," followed by the fragment *There are two trees in a lonely field* (1838) "where "a dreary thought their dark boughs yield/All waving solemnly."[97] The extremes of nature and its complexities would have been studied many times over the years by Emily Bronte, as she ventured out onto the often forbidding landscape of the Yorkshire moors, but, as Charles Simpson pointed out, "Emily cared little whether the moors greeted her with storm or sunshine. She was as happy in an East wind that cracked the nerves of others, as she was in the mystical glow of a winter sunshine."[98]

Music was a major element in the poetry of Emily Bronte, as it had been for the German Romantic poets, who alluded to the condition of music in their work. The art of music has been created by man throughout time, in one form or another. Music has never differentiated between nations or time periods. It has always been timeless and aesthetically pleasing, as well as being adaptable for all events and purposes. However, during the late eighteenth and early nineteenth centuries, subtle changes in the world of music occurred, when Romanticism emerged, and brought with it a new freedom of expression, in which musicians were proud to represent their countries with a new national spirit. Madame de Stael, on her visit to Germany commented that "all Germans were musical......at times, entering a humble smoke-blackened dwelling, I found not only the housewife but also her husband improvising on the spinet, just as Italians improvise poetry...she bought a mouth organ and, during her two days' stay at Gotha, took lessons in playing that humble instrument. The image of Madame de Stael, stately in low-cut dress and turban crowned, blowing upon a harmonica on her way to see Goethe and Schiller, is expressibly endearing."[99]

Germany was the influence behind the new wave as its poets, writers and musicians aimed at composing works that could only be described as dramatic; emotions and feelings inspired composers to reach the heights of sublimity through their works. Most of all, music was freed from any confines or reason but became much more personal and spiritual. It could deeply affect the mood of a listener by its artistic expression. As Gregory Mason pointed out, "there is often a feeling of relief, of freer breathing and ample leisure, as when we leave the confusion of the city for the larger peace of the country."[100]

On the analysis of music, he continued, "every great melody has an indefinable distinction, a sort of personal flavour or individuality, which we discern, but cannot analyze. It has, also, however, an organic quality, depending upon the unity and variety of its phraseology, that we can to a certain extent study and define."[101] With regard to form and structure, Mason claimed that "none of the romantic composers attained a breadth, diversity, and solidity of construction in any wise comparable to Beethoven's."[102]

Stevie Davies suggested that the German influence on Emily would have been reinforced by her stay in Brussels, where Beethoven had "dominated the musical world," and where she would have had the opportunity to hear his symphonies and overtures.[103] Robert K. Wallace concluded that "to Beethoven himself it was obvious that music and literature could inhabit the same emotional, spiritual and stylistic realms. In 1823 he declared that his musical ideas [were] roused by moods, which in the poet's case are transmuted into words, and in mine into tones that sound, roar and storm until at last they take shape for me as notes."[104] Wallace found many similarities between Beethoven and Emily in their expression of the Romantic style. Beethoven's themes and rhymes are equally permeated by the elemental forces of nature,

'I could almost grasp them in my hands,' he said, 'out in nature's open, in the woods, during my promenades, in the silence of the night, at the earliest dawn."[105] Nature provided the inspiration for Beethoven in much the same way as Emily 's vision, combining the spiritual with the mystical.

Charles Simpson stated that "Beethoven was in a sense a mystic. An inscription said to have been taken from the Temple of Isis was always before him on his desk; 'I am that which is – I am all that is, and all that shall be – no mortal man hath my veil uplifted."[106] The philosophy of the inscription could also have belonged to Kant, with its subjective 'I.' However, Beethoven would have strengthened Emily's links with European culture and served as a role model on which to base her writing, with music providing a very powerful and emotional language indeed.

According to Robert K. Wallace, musical life in Brussels in 1842 "was exceedingly rich and varied. The Conservatoire Royal was the centre of serious symphonic life. In April 1842 Emily would have had the opportunity to hear

Beethoven's Seventh Symphony in which, according to one critic in the

L' Independant newspaper "everything [was] beautiful, majestic, sublime, in this

work of genius [which] brought tears to the eyes."[107] Philip Barford, in his study of

Beethoven's late piano sonatas turned to Emily's poem *The Prisoner* for an analogue

to the spiritual vision expressed by the sublime variations movement that concluded

Beethoven's *Opus 109*. The lines he compared to the music were the following;

> *Music soothes my breast – unuttered harmony,*
>
> *That I could never dream, till earth was lost to me.*
>
> *Then dawns the Invisible; the Unseen its truth reveals.*
>
> *My outward sense is gone, my inward essence feels;*
>
> *Its wings are almost free – its home, its harbour found,*
>
> *Measuring the gulf, it stoops, and dares the final bound.*[108]

The Prisoner was suggestive of mystical experience, since it was dramatic in its quest

for ecstasy and emotional response, but as Charles Simpson pointed out "it [was]

difficult to tell how far the colour of Emily's mind was the result of outward

circumstances, or how far her mind imposed itself on all that was around her."[109]

Music was used to great effect in the poems as they wrung out the last drops of

emotion, "like soft music sighing,"[110] or, as a backdrop to create atmosphere, "I hear

the Abbey bells ringing/And wafts its music from my ear."[111] Music was also

personified as in "to my spirit, Old guitar,"[112] and "Harp in other earlier days/I could

sing to thee.[113] Nature's musical qualities were often evoked as the "stream sings

merrily,"[114] and "where the north wind is raving,"[115] or, even in a lullaby, "yet you must know in infancy/Sweet voices to my slumber sung/and music soothed me.[116]

Most of the poems contained musical references in some form, which would have stemmed from Emily's own enthusiasm for playing the piano, and the encouragement she received in Brussels. Natural rhythms and musical qualities could be traced in all the poems, whether simply in the images and sounds of nature, or employing a whole symphony during periods of high intensity, and it could be noted how the poems became songs, even by the titles themselves; Song by... or, Song to... or, having songs merged into the poems, "I said go gentle singer/thy wooing voice is kind/But do not think its music/Has the power to reach my mind," or, "had I known they'd waken woe/I'd weep their music to recall."[117]

Winifred Gérin referred to Emily's musical abilities and noted how Ellen Nussey recalled Emily playing the piano "with precision and brilliancy." Nussey also told us that after Emily returned from Brussels the family acquired a new piano and "the ability with [which] Emily took up music was amazing; the style, the touch, and the expression was that of a professor absorbed heart and soul in his theme."[118] They also acquired *The Musical Library*, an eight volume anthology of instrumental and vocal music published as a collected edition by Charles Knight in 1844.[119]It was no surprise that Beethoven's music was especially taken up by Emily, "her assimilation of his music and his legend in the 1840's sets in a new light the time lag between the Romantic equilibrium he achieved at the beginning of the Romantic age in music, and she achieved near the end of the Romantic age in literature."[120]

The art of music has been created by man throughout time, in one form or another. Music has never differentiated between nations or time periods. It has always been timeless and aesthetically pleasing, as well as being adaptable for all events and purposes. However, during the late eighteenth and early nineteenth centuries, subtle changes in the world of music occurred, when Romanticism emerged, and brought with it a new freedom of expression, in which musicians were proud to represent their countries with a new national spirit.

CHAPTER THREE: The German Romantics: Poetry

According to L.A Willoughby, "each nation must live out its own spirit, must create

its own individual forms of language, religion, society, art and literature, and thus

help enrich the hum

an race as a whole."[1] It was out of such national spirit that German Romanticism was

born. Goethe, Schiller, Tieck and Novalis were amongst the first generation of

Romantic poets from the late eighteenth century, followed by Eichendorff, Brentano

and others. Their revolutionary words reflected human thought and experience in

opposition to any rational or conventional methods usually adopted, and they

embraced the world of the imagination which was to capture and retain the elements

of nineteenth century literature.

Isaiah Berlin attempted to catch the essence of the Romantic move ment, and stated, "whether by external inspection, the most subtle insight so long as they labour under the illusion that it is possible, once and for all to write down, to describe, to give any finality to the process which they are trying to nail down, unreality and fantasy will result – an attempt, always to cage the uncageable, to pursue truth where there is no truth, to stop the unceasing flow, to catch movement by means of rest, to catch time by means of space, to catch light by means of darkness. That is the Romantic sermon."[2] Such comments statement were illuminating, and unlike many other opinions about it, Berlin noted not just the revolutionary aspects, but also what can be the contradictory nature of Romanticism.

Berlin also noted the widespread adoption of romanticism in other countries where there was" some kind of social discontent and dissatisfaction, particularly to countries oppressed…perhaps it found its most passionate expression in England, where Byron was the leader of the entire Romantic Movement, in the sense that Byronism became almost synonymous with Romanticism in the early nineteenth century." He continued "the French Romantics from Hugo onwards are disciples of Byron. Byron and Goethe saw the movement rushing head-on over all obstacles…the waters of the Rhine rise and cover this violent, this chaotic, this unstoppable, this incurable disease by which all mortals are affected. That is the heart of the Romantic Movement in Europe."[3]

An imaginative and extreme form of Romanticism, characteristic of the period, was the Gothic. It brought with it fear and terror from the darkest depths of humanity.

The popularity of Gothic fiction had been a literary phenomenon of the mid-eighteenth and early nineteenth centuries.

The darker side of Romanticism became known as the Gothic element. Dark, over-imaginative with excessive uses of terror and fear; ghosts and supernatural wanderings, medieval castles, churches and graveyards to landscapes and wild, mountainous terrains, and death – the Gothic fiction of imagination and heightened emotional states contained them all, and was very popular with the reading public of the eighteenth and early nineteenth centuries.

Fred Botting provided a condensed historical background to the rise of the Gothic novel, stating that "historically the Gothic was associated with the northern Germanic nations whose fierce avowal of the values of freedom and democracy was claimed as an ancient heritage. Opposed to all forms of tyranny and slavery, the warlike, Gothic tribes of northern Europe were popularly believed to have brought down the Roman Empire. Roman tyranny was subsequently identified with the Catholic Church, and the production of Gothic novels in northern European Protestant countries often had an anti-Catholic subtext."[4]

The major Gothic issues were itemised according to Rictor Norton as being, "the aesthetics of the Sublime, religion and the supernatural, the influence of the ancient romance, the discourse of Enlightenment reason versus Romantic imagination – the hobgoblin machinery of vampires, spectres, orphans, the Inquisition, nuns, storm and ruined castles, labyrinths and mystic forests, alongside social themes of prison reform, revolutionary politics, mother-daughter relationships, illicit sexuality, sensibility and madness."[5] Apparitions and visions appeared as constant members of the Gothic novel, whether to warn or accuse, they always had the capability to terrify.

Willoughby stated that beauty to the Romantics was "synonymous with feeling," (mood and emotion) and that its generating force was "the longing that can only find satisfaction in the chaos of unreality. Its symbol was the blue flower, the colour illustrative of the boundless sky."[6] In German folk-lore the blue flower had the property of opening the eyes of its wearer to the whereabouts of buried treasure," and that it became a potent symbol of German Romanticism projecting an age in which the world becomes dream, dream becomes world and imagination reigns supreme."[7] The effects of the German Romantic Movement and its appreciation were considerable, and Thomas Carlyle called Goethe 'his master,' believing that Goethe had "found serenity by solving for himself the eternal riddle of the relations between man and the universe…by cutting out of his life anything likely to disturb him."[8] One factor often mentioned in the popular rise of German literature in England was Madame de Stael's book, *De L'Allemagne*, published in London in 1813, which was" a great success and sold out completely in three days."[9] The book revealed the Germans to be "civilised by Christianity, and their history is that of the middle-ages, Gothic rather than classical."[10] De Stael discussed the word 'Romantic' and applied it to poetry by relating it to,

"The traditions of chivalry and Christianity…the literature of the ancients is a transplantation, the literature of romance and chivalry is indigenous, national, blossoming under our religion and our institutions and in our modern nations. These are some of the ideas which the Romanticists were to illustrate in their future work…spurring on the growing Romantic impulse of her times…the German poet (comprehending) nature, not only as a poet, but as a brother."[11]

Her words of admiration for German literature were to have a marked effect upon its reception and appreciation in England. The book was reviewed several times, especially voicing its opinions about Goethe and Schiller. Of Goethe, she wrote, "that he could represent all German literature because he alone united all the elements which distinguish the German mind; his writing demonstrated a great depth of ideas, grace born of imagination, and a sometimes fantastic sensitivity."[12]

Matthew Arnold had also become an admirer of Goethe, although much later in the century, and copied a saying of Goethe's into his notebook, "the highest happiness is to find what it is that holds the world together within,"[13] which echoed the words of Fichte, who acknowledged and celebrated the spiritual 'reality' of the universe. His relationship to Romanticism was in the ideology of freedom and the importance of consciousness – inward reflection and reasoning, plus, the image of God being linked to everyday moral activities and experiences. Fichte's influence in England was more slowly felt than Kant's, but Fichte had influenced the Jena University group of philosopher-poets, where the beginnings of the Romantic Movement were centred.

Jena was known as "a modern Athens, and was alive with the writings of Goethe, Schiller, Schelling, Hegel, Schlegel, Hebart, Oerstead and Holderlin."[14] Although they did not share any common ground other than Romanticism, it was said to be "a spiritual forest fire sparked by Fichte's philosophy," freedom being the right of everyone, "the fire only burned when abstract thought was fanned by the wild winds of liberated fantasy and produced a blaze of poetic-philosophic ideas."[15]

The German Romantic poets offered a new perspective of 'Romantic' thought, and yet all dealt with the underlying themes of time, the universe, God and the consciousness of the individual and his destiny. In England there was a Romantic influence where a group of English poets, who have since become known as the Romantic poets or Lake poets, began to voice the concerns of the nation, not just in poetry but in prefaces, theoretical texts and manifestos during the late eighteenth century, through to the first decades of the nineteenth century. Their influence developed as a reaction not only to the French Revolution and European wars, but also to the industrial revolution taking place in England. The English Romantic poets, in similar vein to the Germans, sought to express their feelings within the natural world, recording life how they perceived it. Coleridge was the more radical poet, taking his influences from the German poets the Schelling brothers, Schiller and the philosophy of Kant, which he then introduced into England. He translated Schiller's verse-play *Wallenstein*, and began to plan "a great work on metaphysics."[16]

He openly debated European religious anxiety and produced visionary works such as *Kubla Khan, The Rise of the Ancient Mariner* and *Christabel*. The Gothic-supernatural aspects in many of his works contained all the hallmarks of German Romantic culture, with their dream-like spiritual landscapes of man within nature. It has been said that "Coleridge has perhaps the finest superstitious vein of any person alive," and that the poem *Christabel* was the best model extant of the (Gothic) language fit to be employed for such subjects…and it may be considered as a test by which to try men's feelings of superstition."[17] Coleridge produced many great works and lectured on literature and philosophy, developing his critical ideas "concerning Imagination and Fancy; Reason and Understanding; Symbolism and Allegory; Organic and Mechanical form, Culture and Civilization…expressing his clearest debt to German Romantic philosophy…there is a religious and metaphysical dimension to all his best work, which has the inescapable glow of the authentic visionary."[18]

The German Romantic poet Friedrich von Hardenberg, or Novalis as he became known, was from the early Romantic group established at Jena University. He was influenced by the philosophy of Fichte and the writings of Goethe who, he claimed, "had done for German literature what Wedgwood did for English art.[19] The combination of his study in philosophy and the arts, alongside the sciences of mineralogy, physics and medicine led Novalis to question life and death, and according to Penelope Fitzgerald in her book *The Blue Flower (Die Blaue Blume)* he held "a certain inexpressible sense of immortality."[20] Referring to the French Revolution which had inspired other countries, Novalis commented that "it could be transferred to the world of imagination and administered by poets, believing that "the state should be one family bound by love."[21] It was the subject of love that transformed the life of Novalis, following the death of his greatest love, Sophie von Khün. After her painful death Novalis had an overpowering vision of her as he visited her graveside. He recorded the event in some detail in his journals[22] and his collection of poems, *Hymns to the Night* (1800) and *Spiritual Songs* (1802), followed the strange event in which Sophie and Christ had become an inspiration. He was to perceive the world from then onwards in a new and enlightened way, which stayed with him until his own death a few years later.

"*Hymns to the Night* [told] of the initiation experience that originated with Sophie, and found its way to Christ. In the *Spiritual Songs* the earthly image of Sophie was transfigured by the light of Christ into the heavenly Queen of the World."[23] *Hymns to the Night* could have been described as poems of meditation or reflection on death. They used images of the night to search the spiritual world and, like Emily, the quest for eternity was a powerful force, "aside I turn to the unspeakable, mysterious Night/Afar lies the world."[24] Novalis stated that the night made us aware of ourselves and nature as once, "More heavenly than those glittering stars, we hold eternal eyes which the /Night hath opened within us."[25] The passion for the night quickly evaporated with the morning and the light it brought, which was also expressed by Emily Bronte, "Must the morning always return? /Will the despotism of the earth never cease? /Unholy activity consumes the angel-visit of the Night."[26] For Emily Bronte and Novalis the night brought spiritual comfort, whilst the daylight hours brought the cold reality of everyday existence in a material world. Emily's poem Stars had its analogue with the lines from Novalis, "And hide me from the hostile light/that does not warm, but burn…"[27]

Imagination was the key element to Romantic writings (with its mixture of symbolism and myth) through the medium of nature, "the exploration of subjectivity as a transcendental process, as the unfolding of the mind to itself, as a dynamic quest."[28] Subjectivity for the Romantic poets meant an individual and personal response to which they gave artistic expression and acceptance, that by being open to divine energies they could communicate the eternal and spiritual. Lilian Furst stated that "the Jena group founded their whole system on the unquestioned primacy of the subjective imagination of the original creative genius, a doctrine which had been strengthened by the powerful support of Fichte's philosophy, so that this subjective imagination now became literally the alpha and omega of the universe."[29]

The poetry of Novalis was radically subjective, with its uniquely personal experience of a singular individual. His subjectivism was that outlined in Fichte's *Wissenchaftslehre*. The poetry contained in *Hymns to the Night* [30] could be described as poems of meditation or reflection on death, using the night and the symbol of love to seek the spiritual world. The quest for eternity was the powerful force which drove Novalis on his journey through life. For Novalis, and later Emily Bronte, the "poetic experience was an experience of the absolute, where there exists a sphere of spiritual presence."[31]

The vision and spiritual presence was the central element to the structure of *Hymns to the Night (Hymnen an die Nacht)*. Following the death of his young love, Sophie von Kühn, Novalis poured his feelings into the beautiful and religious lyrics of *Hymns to the Night*.

The inspiration for the poems followed his 'vision' of Sophie when he had visited her grave. The revelation of that event stayed with him for the rest of his life. His perception of the event was an initiation into the spirit world, from Sophie to Christ. A motto which he expressed at the end of his diary read, '*Christ and Sophia.*'[32]

Despite having all the elements of death and dying, the poems were not sad or melancholy, in fact some of them were celebratory where, "the lamps burn lustrous all," with "stars down dripping/Shall flow in golden wine."[33] The triumph of death was the release from death and invitation to eternity, where the happiness he was seeking would culminate in "One jubilating ode/The countenance of God."[34] The poem had the musical rhythmic quality of a song as it moved along happily despite the use of words such as "sorrow-laden,"[35] and "now at no grave are weeping."[36]

The same musical effect can be recognised in the poem *Longing after Death,* its ten-verse format contrasted life and death, past and present. The past was particularly evoked as though it held answers for the future, "The Past wherein still rich in bloom/That blessed time again to know, "but it is the night that will be everlasting."[37]

Night, he realized, had implanted in him an inner eye, "it is an inner light brighter than the light of day, a symbolic night of the soul…Love is the element in which individuals are at one with the transcendental realm, and he longs to reside there."[38] The influence of Novalis and his mystical vision can be seen in the poems of Emily, where consciousness attempts to transcend reality through nature, aiming for that closer union with God, freedom and immortality. The night and the yearning for death were very familiar themes running through the poetry of Emily, and also the curious 'visionary' aspect that both poets adopted, which was through the uncanny, revelations and visions, accompanied by feelings of ecstasy and joy, in an individual and personal response to their own particular need.

Johann Wolfgang von Goethe (1749-1832) captured the essence of man's role in nature when he declared, "if I work on unceasingly till my death, nature is bound to give me another form of being when the present one can no longer sustain my spirit,"[39] which echoed the belief of Novalis that "Life is the beginning of death. Life exists for the sake of death. Death is at once an end and a beginning."[40] The question for both Novalis and later Emily, was whether life was really worth living. An example could be seen in Emily 's poem *The Philosopher*, "O for the time when I shall sleep/Without identity/And never care how rain may steep/Or snow may cover me."[41] The ideas of the German Romantics seem to have been adopted by Emily, who transformed them into her own individual style where, "night and death annihilate space and time, to return to a well-worn theme [by] Novalis."[42]

Goethe was Germany's greatest lyric poet and published frequently in England during the early decades of the nineteenth century. He produced works of a high emotional intensity, being "multifarious in style, form, mood and approach," with images taken from nature, "his lyrics, epic poems, dramas in prose and verse, fiction, autobiography, scientific and miscellaneous writings all became models to emulate."[43] Goethe had been acquainted with Sir Walter Scott, who had translated many of his works, and corresponded with him. Byron had dedicated his play *Werner* (1822) to Goethe, whilst Shelley had been deeply influenced by Goethe, claiming, "I have been reading over and over again *Faust*, and always with sensations that no other composition excites."[44] Harry Blamires commented that "Goethe's early enthusiasm for Shakespeare, for Ossian and for Samuel Richardson, as well as his appreciation of Byron and Scott, involve him in a two-way relationship with English literature."[45] According to Romain Rolland and many other commentators, there had been a female influence in the life of Goethe; Bettina von Arnim. She had served as his greatest influence. It was she who had brought Beethoven and Goethe together. Beethoven had great admiration for Goethe, claiming that "melody [was] the sensual life of poetry,"[46] and asked Bettina for an introduction to him, telling her, "Speak to Goethe of me...With all my heart I long for him to teach me."[47]

The themes of love, music and nature found poetic expression in the poetry of Goethe. A good example could be seen in the poem *Welcome and Farewell* (1789)[48] The landscape of the poem was eerie and intense, suggesting an urgency in the first lines, "My heart beat; at once to horse! The deed was nearly quicker than the thought." Although the rider was alone there was the constant suggestion that nature was his companion, which was personified through the lines, "As blackness peered from the bushes/with a hundred dark eyes," the moon looked on and the wind "beats soft wings." The terror of the night which "created a thousand monsters," was replaced by "veins on fire/In my heart what a blaze." The change of mood from terror turned to one of love, with "A rose-coloured springtime atmosphere," which emerged with his love interest. It was a passionate, visual and atmospheric poem encompassing all the elements of Gothic-Romanticism. The night was evoked by Goethe as it had been for Emily and Novalis. His poem *Night Thoughts* [49] (*Nacht*

Gedanken)saw Goethe speaking to the stars as they "shine in splendour," and the "sojournless, eternal hours [that] lead you," could be compared to Emily's poem *Stars*, in which the stars had "glorious eyes," providing a divine vision as "I saw him, blazing still,"[50] while for Novalis, "...the stars were making/Signal with voiced sweet."[51]

Friedrich von Schiller (1759-1805) had been well published in England in the early decades of the nineteenth century. His biography had been written by Thomas Carlyle. The *Life of Schiller (Das Leben von Schiller)* which had further been published in *The London Magazine* (1823-24) and in book form in 1825. Schiller had written poetry and essays, as well as drama, including *Ode to Joy*, which later became the lyrics for Beethoven's *Ninth Symphony*. His poem *Magnitude of the World* (1782) [52] was deeply reflective, with its Romantic qualities of seeking and finding, and where the space was "void of stars," in "the realm of nothingness." Despite being an example of Romantic poetry it had an edge of realism where "I am," "I have," and "I saw," gave the poem firm grounding in the self, as the poet steered a twisted course through life's "lonely path," seeking the roots of creation, "where the boundary stone of Creation stands." The last verse gave a poignant and emotional answer; "before you is infinity," where "Imagination" [can] "Cast a discouraged anchor here!" Schiller's poetry did not attempt to transcend reality, or take on a mystical appearance, but contained a philosophical streak, taking the 'I' from Kant's beliefs, which were controversial at the time. However, peeling back a layer of the poem's structure we could see that the profound message was in the natural scenery, which took the reader to the heights of optimism, only to be left to face reality, questioning whether life and the universe were just an illusion. It was a question that was to plague the Romantic poets and leave a legacy to feed the [later] imagination and beliefs of Emily.

A comparison of Emily 's poem *Anticipation* (1845) with Schiller's *Magnitude of the World* revealed her empathy with the works of Schiller as shades of her philosophical streak began to emerge, where "every phase of earthly joy/Must always fade, and always cloy," compared with Schiller's "world systems," which "whirl after the man who wanders through the suns." Both poets pointed to the alienation of the self from society. Schiller's poet travelled towards infinity, but then realized that eternity or infinity was all in the mind, and as the mind was in the present it would cast its "discouraged anchor." For Emily Bronte, imagination was where she would cast her own "anchor of desire," and she faced eternity philosophically "with looking for *what it is to be.*"[53]

The Romantic poet and critic Ludwig Tieck (1773-1853) was also one of the pioneers of the Romantic Movement, and "for more than five decades his name had been synonymous with German Romanticism."[54] James Hardin claimed, "Tieck was the progenitor of an entirely new genre, the fairy tale...the depiction of the German forest; the integration of hallucinations and dreams, the free play of fancy; and the effacement of the boundary between the rational and the irrational...one of the most successful experiments."[55] the poem *Miracle of Love* (*Wunder der Liebe*, 1804) was a good example of Tieck's innovative style with its setting in a "fantastic fairy-tale world." The recurring theme of the Romantic poetic quest of seeking and finding an essential self occurs with dramatic lyrics of joy and fear balanced against each other, "when the star of love laughs," to "when gloomy clouds pursue one another," within a musical atmosphere amongst the rich scenic colours of night-time. Belief and unbelief was the message as it wove its way through the concluding verse, where the image of Christ's resurrection was used to great visual effect, "Glowing in the most beautiful flame/ It is offered to heaven."[56] The poem carried the hallmark of the Romantic poet with its escape into the world beyond, leaving behind the realities of this world. In that respect it had an affinity with both Novalis and Emily Bronte who captured the same emotions, longings and desires to leave the earthly life, for a glorious resurrection in the next.

The night was a favourite setting for the Romantic poets, from Schiller's "The moon casts a pale silvery-blue glow," to Tieck's "Moonlit magical night," and Emily's "While nightly stars are burning," and from Novalis, "Blest be the everlasting night." All adopt the Gothic setting for their poetic inspiration. There was far less artificial light in earlier times than today, and the night sky, with its stars, moons and planets, provided the ideal backdrop in which to give free reign to the imagination, whether in dreams and nightmares, the supernatural, or in exploring the darker side of the human imagination. The Romantic poems suggested that while we are on earth we are but prisoners caught in the conflict between life and death, and that life is only the journey into the images the mind gives us of Heaven where the 'Fantastic fairy-tale world,' is a plateau between the conscious and subconscious worlds.

Joseph von Eichendorff (1788-1857) was considered to be one of Germany's foremost lyric poets of the later Romantic period. He expressed powerful feelings for nature and "Wrote hundreds of poems, many of which have been set to music by composers such as Schubert, Mendelssohn, Schumann, Wolf and Strauss."[57] According to H.B Garland, Eichendorff was the finest poet to emerge from the German Romantic Movement. Like Goethe and Schiller before him, he did not portray an objective landscape but caught the diverse moods of man in contact with nature, "Catching the mood of the new world, with his profound insights into the human condition."[58] He presented images of the poet wandering through large forests, as well as the "Many faceted symbols for the demonic forces of nature, their modes of expression bordering on both folk-song and fairy tale."[59] Glyn Tegai Hughes claimed that "As Romanticism was dying out, Eichendorff came along to purify and deepen it."[60] The surrounding countryside provided the inspiration for Eichendorff, as it did for Emily, where, "Forest, springs, clouds, respond to human emotions, the nightingale sings the inexpressible; everything is as fairy-tale like as in dreams."[61] J.W Thomas stated that "The essence of German Romanticism is best expressed in the word 'longing,' either for its medieval past or a complete union with nature, often being a longing for death. The 'longing' of Eichendorff was usually for exotic lands and far-away places where, "My heart burns with longing to wander/ In the glorious summer night."[62] The images compared with Emily 's "This dark night has won me/ To wander far away," in her poem *The Wind I Hear it Sighing.*"[63]

Eichendorff's *Moonlit Night* (1830) [64] followed the example set by Tieck's *Miracle of Love* (1804), having the same musical qualities within the natural colourful suggestions of Mother Nature gently nurturing the earth. The landscape is nocturnal, "So starry-clear was the night," and culminated in transcending the world to salvation, "As if I were flying home," where God seems to be present in nature, "In the glimmer of blossoms…through the fields," and in "the forests." The poet used the simplest language to express the soft movement of the verse, where nature was of a divine origin. Night was again a symbolic force for Eichendorff, where the natural world brought with it a sense of peace and unity between God and man. The religious significance of the poem echoed the nearness to and distance from, God, "As my soul spread/Its wings out wide" [and] "flew through the silent regions." The 'silent regions' suggested a past the poet wished to leave behind; the flawed world of mankind, in order to reach eternity and the fulfilment of Romanticism. This was often interpreted as transcendental, but as Glyn Tegai Hughes pointed out, "What excites about Eichendorff is that behind the apparent quiet conventionality, there combine in universal strength the claims of sensuous natural beauty and of the transcendental. The aesthetic demon is there alright, but under firm control."[65]

The same soft lyrical effects could also be found in the poem *Lullaby* by Clemens von Brentano (1778-1842)[66] where sounds were almost whispered, "Softly softly, softly croon/Sing a whispered lullaby." Brentano's atmospheric effects indicated a sense of isolation as, "Those bees around the lime tree/hum, murmur, whisper, trickle." Comparison could be made with Emily 's fragments where, "Cold, bleakly, drearily," was followed by "Sighing, mourning ever more,"[67] and in a further fragment, "Fall leaves fall die flowers away."[68] Brentano was considered to be the most important writer of the Romantic school after Novalis and alongside Eichendorff. To study his lyrics was "To enter a world in which the life of language is all."[69] His lyrical concentration expressed the Romantic view of music as an integral condition of poetry. Poetry's "Enciphering, hieroglyphic nature both reveals and conceals," and is to "Be understood from within the poems themselves as providing much of the energy and haunting character of his work."[70] It was music that became the great ally in the Romantic period, where, "Not only can we hear Beethoven thundering behind it, but so many of its beautiful lyrics have been set to music by Schubert and Schumann, Brahms and Wolf...The German Romantic Movement...walks along a forest track, narrowly between the infinities of music and metaphysics."[71]

According to L.A Willoughby, "It was Hoffmann (after Wackenroder) who was the real prophet of Romantic music...His influence showed itself in the work of Carl Maria von Weber, whose opera *Der Frieschütz* (1820) was the first German opera on a national basis of popular legend and melody, with a music which endeavoured to adapt itself to nature's moods, grave and gay. It is the first attempt to reproduce by musical means sensuous impressions of the German forest...music has become the expression of the whole soul."[72] C.P Magill added that "The German Romantic writers lived through one of the richest periods in the history of European music, it is hardly surprising that many writers and thinkers of the period should have been obsessed by music."[73]

Goethe had a love-hate relationship with Beethoven, according to Romain Rolland, although each admired the talent of the other.[74] They had met in Teplitz in 1812, following which Beethoven composed several musical pieces based on texts by Goethe. L.A Willoughby stated "Beethoven claimed to have the key to ultimate reality…to have access to a super sensual world, which comprehends mankind, but which mankind cannot comprehend."[75] Few poems, however, held greater attraction for composers than Goethe's *Elf King* (Erlköng); few had lent themselves so well to music. "If we shut out the story we should from its very sound, receive an impression of distinct interchanging mood – and this is music. For what is music, at its purest, but the direct transmission of emotion without concrete thought? It also heralds the well-nigh perfect musical setting by Schubert, in which each thought and feeling of the poem is fitted into its exact musical idiom."[76]

The poetry of Tieck was also full of musical effects, combining assonance, rhyme and rhythm to evoke the sounds and moods of music. According to James Hardin, "Who else [but Tieck] could have claimed to have conversed with Mozart, Beethoven, Wagner…"[77] His poem *Rest Sweet Beloved in the Shade* (1796) was an example of a poetry-song as the poet sings to his lady as they rested (after eloping?) The musical interlude took place within the sphere of nature, which was regarded as comforting and safe. Musical words and images interwove throughout the poem; "The grass is whispering…The grove is rustling…The quiet brook…speaking in "melodies" as the golden bees "hum" peacefully.[78] The poetry of Tieck, with its verbal music was later to influence German Romantic poets Brentano, Heine and Eichendorff, who had "Learned to play several instruments and was particularly fond of the violin."[79] Many of his poems have been set to music by composers Schubert, Mendelsohn, Schumann, Wolf and Strauss, and he was said to be impressed by Mozart's Magic Flute. The appeal of Eichendorff's poetry "lies in a perfect union of content and form, embellished by the musicality of his language. Eichendorff more than any other poet was responsible for the discovery that such a musicality existed. That he was aware of its existence can be seen in the poem *Wishing Wand* (Wünschetrute) [80] which was a short four line poem offering the belief that music was all around us, "Slumb'ring deep in everything," and that the "World begins to sing," when they find "The magic word." The magic word for Eichendorff would surely have been 'music.'

Brentano also had considerable musical talent, and it may have because of it that he too sought the various sounds of nature. Like Eichendorff, the musicality of his poems resembled songs and ballads. *The Bridal Song* (1835) [81] contained many verses and accompaniment throughout, with added religious sentiments. According to Stanley Appelbaum the final two lines of the poem "O star and flower, spirit and robe/ Love, sorrow and time and eternity," were a motto of Brentano's and appeared repeatedly in his later works.[82]

Comparing the features from the German Romantics with Emily has revealed the identical strands of man, nature, imagination and the ever desirable goal of infinity. Nature was always ebbing and flowing towards that goal. Musical influences originating from nature upheld the whole structure of the poems, enhancing them with a hypnotic quality, often resulting in a state of transcendentalism. Novalis's *Hymns to the Night* reflected such a philosophy with their fluid forms and tones, their musical rhythmic quality and rhyming schemes, which often had the effect of being sung as, "The stars were making/Signal with voices sweet."[83] Novalis had commented that "And so it is with language – the man who has a fine feeling for its tempo, its fingering, its musical spirit, who can hear with his inward ear the fine effects of its inner nature and raises his voice or hand accordingly, he shall surely be a prophet."[84] The idealised image of the poet and his function by Novalis was to be later reflected in the works of Emily.

The writer and poet Jean Paul, was introduced to the English reading public, first, by De Quincy and then Carlyle in his *Introduction to German Romance*. There appeared to be many similarities in both the life and works of Jean Paul to that of Emily Bronte. Both had lost a parent early in life, and both had grown up in a rural landscape; Emily within the Yorkshire moors and Jean Paul in the contrasting mountainous and forest area of the Fichtelberg in Germany. Like Jean Paul, Emily's life was also influenced by her father and the church. Nature was the powerful release for both writers as they documented all its wonders, leading them to question their own place in the universe and importantly, the question of immortality. Music also played a role in both of their lives, being talented piano players. On a much deeper level music was a disembodied art form and pervaded all Jean Paul's novels, expressing, mysticism, infinity and the celestial world.

Eliza Buckminster Lee translated Jean Paul's letters and documents, forming the *Life of Jean Paul Friedrich Richter*.[85] She claimed it was the appointment of his father as Pastor in Joditz which began to alter the lives of Jean Paul and his parents, and that it was in those idyllic years Jean Paul "received impressions which would follow him through life and influence all his works. Never is he so much at home in his works, as in the little village parsonage and church…the village festivals, the church consecrations, are all dear to his deeply religious spirit."[86]

During those years Jean Paul developed a love for learning, reading, painting, music, and the start of his interest in philosophy. He claimed, "never shall I forget, that which I have never yet related to human being, - the inward experience of the birth of self-consciousness…that inward consciousness. *I am Me* came like a flash of lightening from Heaven and has remained ever since. Then was my existence conscious of itself, and forever."[87]

It could also be identified in his poem called *The New-Years-Night of an Unfortunate Man (Die Neujahrsnacht eines Ungluecklichen)*.[88] The setting for the poem was, as the poem indicated, New Year's Eve; one year ending and a new one beginning, with reflections upon the past and thoughts about the future.

The poem was structured into eight verses, with rhyming couplets; supernatural and Gothic language, the antithesis of the words creating a strong contrast of images; "his dull eyes," "so cold and white," with "groaned," wretchedness and despair, the "worn out frame," the "blighted soul" with "the dark years of agony, remorse, and withering fears."

The romantic image was of the solitary figure (Jean Paul), whose tragic thoughts and reflections echoed nostalgia for the past, within a supernatural context. With great emotion and remorse the solitary figure had become aware of his own mortality, and he looked back to his childhood where "his father placed him first," making choices for him, but that he had to make his own decisions after that. His thoughts about his father caused him pain and to cry out, "Oh, father" be my guide/And let me only choose my path once more." (26:4)

The images of impending death hovered over the poem, as man, nature, and the changing industrial society were also evoked, and the "huge windmills lifted up their arms to crush/And skeleton faces rose up from the dim/Depths of the charnel-house, and glared on him!"(38-40/5) Music, always so special to Jean Paul, provided the antithesis to the sounds of death, as "Softer emotions o'er him now came stealing."(45/6) providing a calming sensation and return to normality."

The poem had a tragic feel as the figure faced death, taking stock of his life, but recognising that it was God who gave him strength and would guide him to choose the right path in his life, "He wept, and thanked his God that, with the will/He had the power to choose the right path still."(56/7) providing a contrast of the spiritual with the consciousness of his mortality.

The poem was based upon the dream Jean Paul had of his own death, which he recalled in the final verses; "...Still was he young, for he had dreamed the whole." (50/7) Followed by the warning, "This ghastly dream may be thy guide to bliss."(60/8)

The conclusion to the poem acted as a warning about the shortness of life to young people, with an instruction to follow the right path, because, "Vainly thy tears may flow above the urn/Of thy departed youth –it never will return."(63-4/8) It was a stark warning and reality to all, that life passes by so quickly, and in the end we have only memories, and perhaps regrets of what might have been had we followed a different path.

CHAPTER FOUR: The German Romantics

and the Novelle

The birth of the Romantic Movement in Germany began in Jena with the philosopher Fichte, who followed Kant's philosophies, and celebrated the spiritual reality of the universe which, in turn, led to a theory of ideas linked to Romanticism. Their ideas were about freedom and the importance of consciousness – inwardly reflecting and reasoning, plus the image of God being linked to everyday moral activity and experience. Jena was known as the "modern Athens, and was alive with the writings of Goethe, Schiller, Schelling, Hegel, Oersted, Herder, and Holderlin."[1] The influence of Fichte in England was more slowly felt that Kant's, but Fichte had influenced the Jena group of philosopher-poets, where the beginnings of the Romantic Movement were centred. Friedrich and August Wilhelm Schlegel founded the German literary journal called *Das Athenaeum*, which was the most influential journal of Romanticism, allowing exposure for emerging poets and writers.

In German literature the novel came in many forms, and the novella (die novelle) came to be recognised as an alternative novel form, but with the novel having much more freedom of movement. Chris Baldick defined the 'novelle' as a "German term for a fictional prose term that concentrates on a single event or situation usually with a surprising conclusion."[2] The term was adopted from the Italian 'novella.' It had been used by Goethe but also in works by Tieck, Kleist, and later by Thomas Mann. E.K Bennett stated that in a novella "the teller of the story often appeared as a definite character within the narrative."[3] Jean Paul was well known for using this technique, putting forward his own opinions within the text. E.K Bennett explained that "in the novelle the action revolved around a striking fateful event which befell a certain person or group of persons: an event which was often of supreme importance in the life of the person concerned [and] of the changes it produced in his life."[4] He illustrated the point by referring to Kleist's novella Michael Kohlhaas whose horses were taken from him and justice refused him. Out of that event was developed the whole action of the novelle. The illustration how, in the novella the passive hero was at the mercy of circumstances which would shape his future fate. Bennett described it as "presentation, not of character as fate, as in the drama, but of chance as fate."[5]

Apart from the tensions of the narrative, Bennett stated the novella could produce a happy or tragic ending. It could also present life as fatalistic, but the one particular aspect of the novelle was its concentration upon the one individual around whom everything else revolved. Bennett distinguished Friedrich Schlegel as being the first theoretical writer on the novella in German literature, and who described it as "an anecdote, a hitherto unknown story, which must be able to arouse interest by itself, without reference to the ordinary course of human culture and history."[6] He pointed out "the possibility of retelling and remodelling already known stories in such a way that they acquire the charm of novelty; and hints here the personality of the narrator may be the real attraction."[7]

Bennett pointed out that it was, in that way, characteristics of the romantic exploitation of the subjective, and that the novella provided a subjective outlet, as the narrator gave the objective details, he could also express his own subjective feelings. Bennett again referred to Kleist and "his desperate uncertainty and questioning attitude to life."[8]

Goethe had attempted to define the novella stating it was "an event which is unheard of, but has taken place."[9] Bennett suggested it was a 'real' definition and that "many German works were labelled as being 'Novelle,' but were actually not."[10] He cited Wieland's definition that the events of the novelle should take place in the real world," confirming that the fantastic did not have a place in the novella, but, as Bennett pointed out, "the Romantics did not always accept that definition, but passed between reality and fantasy."[11]

Paul Ernst, who had written extensively about the novelle form claimed, "the improbable, which may even be intensified to the impossible, is the very atmosphere in which the novella, that sister of the fairy tale, is most at home. It is perhaps the greatest pleasure for the poet, as far as this type of composition is concerned, to represent the improbable in such a manner as to give the impression of the purest probability."[12] Ludwig Tieck also contributed to the debate about the definition of the novelle. In 1829 he stated in his collected works that "the novelle presents in a clear line a happening of greater or less importance, which, however easily it may occur, is yet strange and perhaps unique. This 'twist' in the story, this point from which it takes unexpectedly a completely different direction, and develops consequences which are nevertheless natural and in keeping with character and circumstances, will impress itself the more firmly upon the imagination of the reader, in so far as the story, in spite of its strangeness might under other circumstances be completely commonplace." He added, "a genuine novella may be bizarre, arbitrary, fantastic, witty, garrulous, losing itself completely even in the presentation of side issues, tragic as well as comic; profound and saucy – all of these qualities are possible in the novelle – but it will always have that extraordinary and striking turning point which distinguishes it from every other narrative form."[13] Tieck's definition, despite his comprehensive account named the 'turning point' or 'unexpected twist' as being the most central factor to the novelle.

A further definition by Hyse stated the novella should "present to us a significant human fate, an emotional, intellectual or moral conflict, and that it should reveal to us by means of an unusual happening, a new aspect of human nature...within a restricted framework...impress themselves profoundly upon the memory"[14] As Bennett implied, the theory of Hyse was "not very profound nor very illuminating," and concluded that the novelle must have a definite subject matter and make an impression on the memory."[15]

Romanticism followed hotly on the heels of the many and various theories about the German novel or novella, as writers began to concentrate upon those human aspects so frequently discussed; emotions thoughts, imagination and the total freedom of expression, encouraging a type of universal humanity was born. All previous rigid and classical structures were abandoned in favour of a liberal 'human' and 'naturist' approach. Throughout Europe each country had their own interpretations of Romanticism, whether adopting a forward-looking approach or looking back to the past for answers. Romanticism in its broadest sense, was a search for truth. It was a movement, a reaction to the past, to oppressions and wars, confinement and prejudice, allowing the individual to become aware of himself and his own mortality, to make his own choices, and most of all to give free reign to the emotions.

In England there was an enthusiastic welcome for all things associated with Romanticism. The German writers were given a glowing reference by Thomas Carlyle, who admired the works of Goethe, Schiller and Jean Paul Richter. England adopted Romanticism very early in the nineteenth century prior to the Victorian Age, as the works of the German writers began to pour into the country. Although there were differences and similarities with each country, the German Romantics had a strong regard for the English interpretation, and importance that they too placed upon the imagination.

It was Goethe's *The Sorrows of Young Werther* (*Die Leiden des jungen Werther*), which impressed Madame de Staël, and she commented that it was "one of the most excellent works of the German writers, and which they may just hold up in opposition to the master pieces of other languages…as it is called a romance, many are ignorant that it is a work of higher consideration: and indeed, I am not acquainted with any production that displays a more striking and natural picture of the wanderings of enthusiasm; a deeper insight into misfortune; in a word, a search into that abyss of Nature, where truth displays itself at once to the eye that is capable of discerning it."[16]

Love, passion, madness and suicide were the main themes of both *The Sorrows of Werther* and *Wuthering Heights*, as we followed the trials of central characters; Heathcliff and Werther. The style of presentation differed as Goethe's novel was divided into two sections; book one and book two, but also as an epistolary novel, omitting any replies. Nature was an important aspect for Goethe as it was later for Emily. Werther's experiences seem to be in tune with the changing natural vista, from the early days of his travels when he commented happily how he "looked down into the lovely valley from the hilltop…the grove yonder…that mountain top…those hills linked together and the intimate valleys,"[17] to the later view of nature as a tormentor, "The warm, rich feeling of my heart for living nature, which flooded me with so much rapture, which turned the world around me into a paradise, is now becoming an unendurable tormentor to me."[18] He continued to "monstrous mountains [and the] abysses [which] lay before me…what undermines my heart is the consuming power which lies hidden in the whole of nature."[19] The onset of Werther's madness became apparent as he raved about the overpowering force of nature, "I see nothing but a monster which, eternally swallowing, chews its eternal cud."[20]

The theme of obsessive love was one exploited by Emily Bronte through Heathcliff and Cathy in her novel *Wuthering Heights*, whilst Goethe's character Werther found himself falling deeper in love with Lotte, knowing that his love could never be returned when she married Albert. His obsession gradually drove him to the brink of insanity, and instead of walking away he chose to stay and suffer, being unable to leave the object of his affections, declaring his thoughts of "in this torn heart the frenzied thought has slunk about, often – to murder your husband! Or you! Or me!"[21] Werther's suicide, like that of Heathcliff was the ultimate solution for both Romantic heroes.

Schiller and Kleist were influenced by Kant, but their writing had marked differences of interpretation; Schiller's characters were strong and had the power of the human will, whilst Kleist's novels showed his characters being unable to understand their predicaments, displaying weakness and inability to make sense of situations. Ultimately, the result is manipulation by evil external powers.

These are evident in his tragedies; *Robert Guiskard* (1808), *Die Familie Schroffenstein* (1803), *Penthesilea* (1808) and his comedy *Amphitryton* (1807); the latter dealing with loss of self-awareness, and despite its cover being as a comedy, it also has its tragic side.

Thomas Mann claimed that Kleist was "one of the greatest, boldest, and most ambitious poets Germany has produced; a playwright and storyteller of the very first order."[22] Unfortunately, he had always felt the pressure of having to compete with Goethe and Schiller. Thomas Mann stated that Kleist had an "ambivalent attitude to Goethe, forever oscillating between humility and hatred, admiration and fierce jealousy."[23] Mann pointed out that "there [was] nothing else in our literature as loftily beautiful as Goethe's *Iphigenia*" [and] that "there could be no more successful formal experiment than Schiller's imitation of classical drama in the *Bride of Messina*."[24]

St. Cecilia could be classed as a Gothic tale, with its psychological and cold approach to the subject matter. It was one of Kleist's novellas and, as Martin Greenberg pointed out, "the suspense of his stories [was] positively alarming. We are filled with anxiety and terror [and] shudder in the face of mystery, doubt in the powers of reason and, indeed, in the power of God himself—all our affects are confounded."[25] It is a very atmospheric story in which Kleist makes the reader smell the incense and hear the hypnotic music, against the sinister threat, in full Gothic terror, to the nuns. It is a very good example of the power of good triumphing over evil. Kleist's novels often contain the question of God and his powers. The Catholic Church had an uneasy effect upon Kleist, who could never work out if there was some form of magic used, or if there was indeed a God who could bring retribution and damnation. The conclusion of the story highlights his concern when the perpetrators are left with a terrifying affliction; spending their remaining days repeating the *Gloria in excelsis.*

Kleist's conclusion to the story questions the actions of the Catholic Church; does it employ magic or is there a genuine divine intervention? Should people embrace the Church or fear it? The one truth, however, in this story was that good not only outwitted evil, but it also exacted its revenge.

Kleist's search for the truth alongside guilt and innocence followed the lines of Romanticism. Martin Greenberg stated that "in his early youth [Kleist] was a student of the Enlightenment and a devotee of reason. Then he read Kant's philosophy [and] underwent a profound crisis of the spirit…to question the traditional and the rational, the traditions and the reasons of civilization."[26]

Kleist's own life could be described as a tragedy, as he sought encouragement and recognition from his peers. Joachim Maass stated that "although what sometimes seems Christian in his thinking was in reality a sacred but pagan awe of the world's unfathomable mysteries. Hope and faith were not in his character; he had only his experiences to go by, and that was discouraging."[27] He appeared to have a death wish and was drowning in depression and unhappiness. Despite the success of many of works he never found peace or the acceptance he was seeking, and took his own life at the age of thirty

The author, Hoffmann, was recognised for his contribution to German literature, and received some quite stern criticism from Thomas Carlyle, when the novels of the former were reviewed in England. A colourful character, Hoffmann had displayed some artistic and musical tendencies alongside those of his writing throughout his life. Although intent upon being a writer early in his life, he was discouraged by the lack of interest in his first two novels, due, he was told, to his anonymity. After a move to Poland, where he discovered the "strong Hungary wine,"[28] and several ventures which ended in disaster, he finally returned home to Berlin, where he wrote a collection of essays called *Fantasiestücke in Callot's Manier (Fantasy-pieces in the style of Callot),* with its *Preface* being written by Jean Paul Richter. He found fame following the popularity of his essays, but with the Napoleonic wars always in the background, his fortunes were always in danger. Following the success of his essays he published *Elixiere des Teufels* (*Devil's Elixir*),

This was later translated into English. He was excluded from Berlin literary society because of his abruptness and ill manners.

Hoffmann returned to the demon of drink that he had discovered in Poland, and from there, "the tavern was his study, and his pulpit, and his throne: here his wit flashed and flamed like an Aurora Borealis, and the table was for ever in a roar; and thus, amid tobacco smoke, and over coarse earthly liquor, was Hoffmann wasting faculties which might have seasoned the nectar of the gods."[29]

He published the novel *Nachtstucke* (Night-Pieces), a further four volumes of 'Tales' as well as the *Tom-Cat Murr's Philosophy of Life.* Despite suffering a long painful illness, Hoffmann managed to write his final novel *Der Feind* (*The Enemy*).

Carlyle's final words about Hoffmann to his English readers were far from complimentary, stating that "from all this there grew in Hoffmann's character something player-like, something false, brawling and tawdry, which we trace both in his writing and his conduct. His philosophy degenerates into levity, his magnanimity into bombast: the light of his fine mind is not sunshine, but the glitter of an artificial firework."[30] Carlyle concluded that "as in Art, so in Life, he had failed to discover that agreeable sensations are not the highest good. His pursuit of these led him into many devious courses, and the close of his mistaken pilgrimage was – the tavern."[31]

However, having been so critical of Hoffmann he did admit that "His genius formed the most important element of his character, and of course participated in its faults."[32] Carlyle admitted that Hoffmann was "not to be overlooked in any survey of German literature, and least of all by the foreign student of it."[33] Hoffmann had been a keen student of philosophy, as well as literature and had attended the lectures of Kant.

Much of Hoffman's inspiration had come from the other Romantic writers he had encountered in Germany, particularly Jean Paul, and according to Robert Herdon Fife, "Thus so far no one seems to have undertaken a careful search through Hoffmann's published works and such letters and fragments of his diary as have seen the light for elements which may have been due to vivid and persistent impressions derived from the early and constant reading of Richter."[34]

Herdon Fife referred to Hoffman's darker moments when he had 'fled' to

Richter, "during his lonely childhood and amid the storm and stresses of the unfortunate love affair with Cora Hatt."[35] But, in support of Hoffmann, Hendon Fife claimed, "in view of his devotion to Rousseau, to Goethe's *Werther* and to Richter, it is not surprising his first efforts were in romantic form…in the general nature of its contents and form, it reminds one strongly of certain portions of the *Hesperus*."[36] He continued to comment upon Hoffmann's admiration for Richter, but also upon Jean Paul's observations of Hoffmann as he "attached himself to the circle of Romanticists."[37]

The Romanticists at Weimar "could make no headway against the broad flood of sentimentality with which Richter swept on the youthful and especially the feminine part of the reading public…[and] although going their own path, recognised Jean Paul tacitly, or with grudging openness, as one of themselves in many ways."[38] His romances contained the dual personality, second self or doppelgänger; Leibgeber in *Siebenkäs* re-appeared as Schoppe in *Titan*, just as the hero Kreisler appeared in the early fantasies, and again in *Kater Murr*. "In addition to their personal note or background, a literary original can be shown for nearly all of Hoffmann's stories; it is more than probable, therefore that the permanent humorous figure, at least in cellular form, owes its origin to Richter."[39]

Hoffmann's works, again following the path of Jean Paul, contained music. Hoffman had been a keen musician as well as writer, and so it would seem natural for him to indulge his passion, and incorporate it where he could into his novels. In his first volume of *Fantasiestüke* the themes are predominantly musical. The 'inner music' used by Jean Paul was also taken for Hoffmann's *Ritter Gluk* and his *Kreisler*, and ranged from demonic to angelic tones.

When discussing the uses of irony by both authors, Herdon Fife suggested that "we find here Hoffmann and the Romanticists in general, had a forerunner, or at least a disciple in Richter [and that] Jean Paul operates with the same methods as Lawrence Sterne, on the one side; and that on the other hand, Tieck and Brentano have developed Jean Paul's gentle irony into an engine of distortion and destruction."[40]

Hendon Fife concluded that "Goethe, Rousseau, and Schiller, half-forgotten writers like Grosze, and the humorists, Sterne, Lichtenberg, and Hippel, not to speak of the Romanticists, may be held responsible either individually or as collective groups, for many traits in Hoffmann…Jean Paul exercised a considerable influence on Hoffmann, not merely in sentimental moments, but in the formation of his satirical-ironical note as well, [but living close to Richter] the patterns found in the Jean Paul novels could be seen in Hoffman's Kreisler, as well as the doppelgänger motive."[41]

Herdon Fife presented a strong case against Hoffmann, and his taking the ideas and work of Jean Paul to use as his own. He stated, "Richter's style on Hoffmann appears incontestable, but that Dr Ellinger, one of Hoffmann's main biographers and editors, claimed that although Richter's influence was a part of Hoffmann's development, the main influence was that of the Romanticists."[42]

Jeremy Adler, in his Introduction to *The Life and Opinions of the Tom Cat*

Murr, commented that in Russia too, "Pushkin as a story-teller as well as Gogol and Dostoevsky likewise testify to Hoffmann's influence [and that] his contributions are often overlooked. In Italy too, Italo Calvino's narratological pyrotechnics, Garcia Marquez's century of solitude and Umberto Eco's fantastical monastery all betray recognizable Hoffmannesque traits."[43] Whatever may have been said about Hoffmann by his fellow-writers, his works have always remained and been referred to over the years. *The Nutcracker* was the inspiration for the ballet by Tchaikovsky, and *The Sandman* became the focus of the *Uncanny* by Sigmund Freud.

The themes of immortality, providence and fate, coupled with human existence, were taken up by fellow writers Goethe, Tieck and Jean Paul. Jean Paul Richter was a German author writing at the turn of the 18th century and early years of the 19th century. He was often remembered as being a writer of the Romantic Age, alongside authors such as Goethe and Schiller. However, despite the popularity of Goethe and the other Romantic poets and writers of the age, Jean Paul Richter was very individual and unique in his style. George Stuart Collins, in the introduction to his book *Selections from the Works of Jean Paul Friedrich Richter*, stated that the other writers, and even his friend Herder, "never seem to have been in full sympathy with the trend and work of his mind."[44] Indeed, his mind was a rare and unique one that never rested. He would study everything around him, and was fully aware of the emerging trends in literature from England, France and Italy. He observed people and incorporated them, especially the women, into his novels. His style of writing included reflections of his own life, allowing him to appear in different guises in many of his novels, as well as the digressions where he could make observations about people and situations.

Jean Paul Richter had been a much loved writer and poet not just by his fellow countrymen, but also by Carlyle in England, who promoted his works, recommending him to the British public. Throughout his books, Jean Paul had the same philosophy of contrasting the real with the ideal. For him, chasing the ideal, would meet with confusion and disappointment, which reflected upon his own life in many ways. He would always return to the simplicity of nature and life, his observations of humanity, and which led to his own philosophy of sentimentalism, which was a form of emotion but coupled with humour; a type of warmth which radiated throughout his works, using words that his countrymen could empathise with.

The many novels of Jean Paul included *The Invisible Lodge*, *Hesperus*, *Titan*, and *Flower, Fruit, and Thorn Pieces*, and the *Immortality of the Soul*, amongst other shorter works and poetry. It was also Jean Paul who introduced the term 'doppelgänger,' a device he incorporated into his novel *Flower, Fruit and Thorn Pieces* through Siebenkas and his doppelgänger Leibgeber.

Like Patrick Bronte, Jean Paul suffered in later years with blindness, a theme he adopted many times in his novels, only to succumb to the condition himself. Jean Paul had been popular in German during his writing years as an active participant in the Romantic circles, but sadly his fame has been sadly overlooked over the years.

Tieck was one of the pioneers of the Romantic Movement, and for more than five decades his name was linked to German Romanticism. He was "the progenitor of an entirely new genre, the fairy tale…the depiction of the German forest; the integration of hallucinations and dreams, the free play of fancy; and the effacement of the boundary between the rational and irrational…one of the most successful experiments."[45]

Tieck, whose first three novels were described as being 'gloomy' and 'tragic,' by Thomas Carlyle, proved his critics wrong when he published his *Volkmährchen (Popular Tales).* The response of Thomas Carlyle was glowing with praise as he told his English readers that "the active and positive of Goodness was displacing the barren and tormenting negative; and worthy feelings were now being translated into their only proper language, worthy actions."[46] He continued, "In Tieck's mind, all goodness that was noble or excellent in Nature, seems to have combined itself under the image of Poetic Beauty; to the service and defence of which he has ever since unweariedly devoted his gifts and his days." Carlyle found Tieck's Tales to be "of the most varied nature: sombre, pathetic, fantastic, satirical; but all pervaded by a warm, genial soul [and] a starry splendour twinkles down from the immeasurable depths of Night."[47] It was with that reference that Carlyle introduced Tieck to the English reader.

The translation into English of Tieck's *Der Gestiefelte Kater* (a dramatised version of *Puss in Boots*) gave an insight into the character by Carlyle, "he had laughed with his whole heart, in a true Aristophanic vein, at the actual aspect of literature…it rained like a quiet shower of volcanic ashes on the cant of illumination, the cant of Sensibility, the cant of Criticism [and] where pit and stage, where man and animal, and earth and air, are jumbled in confusion worse confounded, and the copious, kind, ruddy light of true mirth overshines and warms the whole."[48]

Tieck later married and moved to Jena where he became friends with the Schlegel brothers, Novalis, Goethe and Schiller. Together they created the New School of Poetry. Carlyle commented that "for the principles of German poetics, we can only refer the reader to the treatises of Kant, Schiller, Richter, the Schlegels..."[49] Tieck's other works included *The Kaiser Octavianus* and *Die Gernälde* (*The Pictures*) which were very popular in Germany and translated into English. Carlyle spoke about Tieck's visit to London and summed him up as being "a Poet born as well as made [with] a still imagination, in the highest sense of that word."[50]

The German Romantics sought an alternative reality, through the natural and celestial worlds of God and nature. The vast landscape with its ever-changing seasons, its eternal wanderer, life, love and musical atmospheres were all ingrained in both poetry and fiction, with that most elusive element of death at its core. Music was also often used, being able to create heightened emotional effects. It was through meditation and the seeking of immortality and God that all barriers of realistic thought were broken. Death and existence allowed the Romantics to break through those barriers of reality to explore the spiritual world, and were clearly visible in the works of Emily Bronte.

CHAPTER FIVE: German Women

Survey with me, what ne'er our fathers saw,

A female band despising NATURE'S law,

As 'proud defiance' flashes from their arms,

And vengeance smothers all their softer charms.[1]

Although much recognition has been given to the German writers and poets over the years, recent research has shown the women writers of Germany had also been busy creating their own literatures. Overlooked for many years it seems appropriate to include some of those whose names can be included in the canon.

Between the years of the late eighteenth century and the advent of Bronte writings, both English and German authors and poets were producing some outstanding artistic and literary works. Women's writing had previously been confined to the areas of letters, minor poetry, travelogues and sentimental fiction for a primarily female circle of friends. Women held meetings to discuss all social matters, they corresponded frequently, commenting on the Romantic theories and works. Friedrich Schlegel's philosophy stated that "dialogue in particular [was] considered to be the underlying principle of Romantic thinking, [having] multiple perspectives, i.e. opinions and views."[2]

In England at the beginning of the nineteenth century the influential female poets Anna Barbauld, Anna Seward, Charlotte Smith and Mary Robinson were also making their mark. The poet and writer Anne Radcliffe had emerged to challenge the male Gothic writers with both her poetry and novels, the themes of which were often dark and sinister, thwarted ideal love of the hero and heroine, medieval castles and monasteries against a foreign and often cold, bleak, mountainous setting.

In Germany, as in other countries, the female writer had been marginalised during the Romantic era, but female poets and writers who escaped from the fringes of society to become recognised included Annette von Droste-Hülshoff (1797-1845), Johanna Schopenhauer, (1766-1838), Bettina von Arnim (1785-1859), Caroline de la Motte Fouque (1775-1831), Rahel von Varnhagen (1771-1833), Benedikt Naubert (1756-1819), and Sophie Albrecht (1757-1840).

The literary output of the women writers and poets coincided with that of the main male Romantics, and the 'salons' or meeting places were useful for them to exchange ideas and get feedback for their own individual works, which represented their beliefs, status and nationalism. Although the writings of women were regarded as 'domestic,' as opposed to their more highly academic male counterparts, they produced works which also contained political motives and questions, including challenges and protests about the situation of women and their stereotypes.

Goethe questioned "but shouldn't intelligent and talented women be able to acquire intelligent and talented male friends to whom they could show their manuscripts, so that all unfeminine traits would be expunged and nothing would remain in such a work which would depart from natural feeling...like a burdensome counterweight" He had also offered the following review of another female novel, claiming that, "Epic and semi-epic writing demands a main character which will be introduced by a man in the case of dominance of the action, by a woman in the case of the dominance of suffering."[3] Goethe's words simplified his opinions about women writers into two spheres; action (men) and suffering (women). Despite his earlier conviction that intelligent and talented women should not only take the advice of male authors, but also rid their work of any link to the feminine, he overlooked the obvious fact that women writers would attract women readers! Again, Goethe's attitude whilst on the surface being supportive of women, still refused to acknowledge women in the field of literature.

For Goethe and his colleague Friedrich Schlegel, women's nature and situation dictated their position. Schlegel stated that "it is not the destiny of women which is domestic, it is their nature and situation. And I consider it more a useful than a happy truth, that even the best marriage, motherliness itself and the family can entangle them and degrade them so easily with the needs of economy and the earth, that they no longer remain mindful of their divine origin and image."[4] The woman writer, in his opinion, cannot aspire to the 'imaginative' world created by the male writers due to them being mothers, wives and everything that is domestic or feminine. Such double standards when the male poet and writer would portray women as 'idealised' muses in their own works. The world of 'Mother Nature,' however, was one in which the female poet and writer could relate to, and one in which held the ultimate power over all.

Despite being confined to the edges of the literary world, German women continued to write, and as Romanticism progressed they found more support, gaining eventual recognition in the 1820's by Carl Wilhelm von Schindel who produced a three-volume bibliography of German women writers of the nineteenth century.[5]

Annette von Droste-Hülshoff was very much the German equivalent in many ways to Emily Bronte. Their backgrounds had a similar spiritual and environmental outlook, both appreciating music and ability to play the piano. Both had moors as their surroundings, with nature and God as the inspiration for their powerful and emotive poetry. Although Annette had been born into a more aristocratic family background, she had led a quiet, sheltered and reclusive life. Her father, like Patrick Bronte, had provided a well-stocked library where, like Emily Bronte, she would have spent many hours reading. She had been devastated when her father died. He had "encouraged in his daughter a love of nature...a kinship with natural things, animals and plants, and a response to landscape, the elements and the importance of the changing seasons and times of day…"[6] He would have been interested and proud of Annette's literary talent, whilst her mother did not seem to understand, only repaying Annette's first attempts with silence. It had been especially hurtful as Annette had found herself floundering in a spiritual wilderness and needed support and encouragement. She penned the poem *Das geistliche Jahr* (1820),

> And see, I looked for thee with pain,
>
> Where could I find my God and King?
>
> Not in my heart, now dead again,
>
> Thine image vanished though all my sin.
>
> Yet all around resounds my cry to thee,
>
> And, as in jest, it echoes back to me."[7]

Interestingly, Marion Tymms in *The Wild Muse* noted that the characteristics of Annette "were something of an enigma…a mass of contradictions in many respects, sociable and open, yet almost crippled by her introspection and guarded in what she chooses to disclose." Such a description could have been, and often was applied to Emily Bronte. Further, Marion Tymms stated, "Annette appears to have enjoyed a more domestic companionship, her warmth and hospitality counteracted by an aloofness and awkwardness which was often referred to and which possibly, to the end of her life, militated against easy social exchange. [Her family] clearly saw aspects of her personality which were concealed, perhaps deliberately, from a wider circle."[8] Those insightful words resonate strongly with the personality of Emily Bronte, who displayed the same spectrum of characteristics, and which would provide for an interesting psychological assessment.

The novel by Annette called *Ledwina* could have been an autobiographical reflection of her own life as the character of Ledwina displayed "a profound sense of isolation both physical and emotional. The following lines from the poem *The Portrait* also has a troubled theme with the distress and confusion of seeing the world through eyes in a unique way,

> I will not look at that which is unfamiliar,
>
> I do not wish to know where it burns,
>
> Whether on the lip or on the eyebrows,
>
> That flame which does not know your heart.
>
> I wish only to look into your eyes,
>
> Take in only that one pure look
>
> Which silently speaks my name.[9]

Annette von Droste-Hülshoff has been remembered as one of Germany's greatest poets, but a novel she had written *The Jew's Beech* (*Die Judenbuche)* has been compared to *Wuthering Heights* because of its Westfalian landscape, environment and atmosphere. Bennett had described it as a "distinctive type of the German Novelle; all that Goethe, Kleist and the Romantics had contributed to the creation of a new form: realism enriched by poetical depth and symbolic significance."[10] He described Droste-Hulshoff as "a lyrical poetess, whose descriptions of Westphalian landscape have a quality which no other German lyrical poetry possess…[and that] "The characters of the stories are so closely connected with the definite locality in which they are set, that their very existence appears to be conditioned by it."[11] It was the only prose work ever to be completed. Eckelmann stated that it was a story "briefly and brilliantly told – the maximum of content in the minimum of space. It embodies visual imagination of the highest order." Her grandfather had told Annette the story when she was a child. Eckelmann added that the walk through Brede forest "was wonderful in its weird beauty…a symbolic setting [which] foreshadows the future."[12] Bennett added that both the Romantic and the later Novellen owe a great deal to irrational elements; but in Droste-Hulshoff's work the irrational is not exploited for its own sake [but] asserts itself as an ethical factor, appearing as the force which drives the murderer back to the scene of his crime and compels him to expiate it by a voluntary death."[13]

As in Wuthering Heights, *Die Judenbuche*, was a story connected to and conditioned by its surroundings. It contained elements of realism in its subject matter, but also recognisable traits of Romanticism in its spiritual, psychological and emotional expression.

When reading the simple nature poem, *The Pond*, (*Der Weiher*) by Drost-Hulshoffe one can imagine the smile it would have brought to the face of Emily Bronte. Indeed, if we had not known that the poem originated in Germany it would have been so easy to guess it as having been penned by Emily Bronte, with its artistic technique, drawing each aspect of its subject into a masterpiece. The central theme of a pond at daybreak captures the beauty and silence of a new day.

> *It lies so quietly in the light of dawn,*
>
> *As peaceful as a pious conscience;*
>
> *When western winds its surface kiss*
>
> *The lakeshore's flower does not feel it;*
>
> *Dragonflies quiver above it,*
>
> *Little rods of blue-gold and carmine,*
>
> *And on the sun- reflection's gleam*
>
> *The water spider does his dance;*
>
> *At the shore wreaths of iris stand*
>
> *And harken to the bulrush's lullaby;*
>
> *A gentle rustling comes and goes*
>
> *As though it whispered: Peace! Peace! Peace!-*[14]

Caroline de La Motte-Foque (1773-1831) was a prominent female writer and friend to the main Romantic male poets and writers. She took inspiration from them using the elements from the spiritual world and its images in her works, whilst adding her own unique view of the world in over twenty novels and many short stories. Her second husband, Friedrich de la Motte Foque was a popular author. His novels, such as *Undine* (1811) centred upon the romance of chivalry in a romantic medieval past.

Although women were not encouraged to voice opinions about politics and worldly affairs, in contrast to her husband Caroline's observations often led her to make social comments through her works. Her opinions about the French Revolution in *Magic der Natur: Revolutions- Geschichte* (*The Magic of Nature: Story of the Revolution*) (1812) resulted in the family's exile to Switzerland and then Germany. In her novel *The Heroin from the Vendee* (*Das Heldmädchen aus der Vendee* (1816) in which German volunteers fought to fend off Napoleonic occupation, she stated, "Truth is the most important thing. No poetry achieves greater things than what the profound seriousness of history reveals to us…But the outcomes of the past and the future are connected individually in an often incomprehensible manner…The hieroglyphs look at us dimly at times. Despairingly we invoke the help of fantasy that animates the soul of life with its moving breath…This is how shape, colour, development, context and even the reproduction of historical life emerges from the history of the world."[15]

The novels of Caroline de la Motte Fouque relied upon a central male hero, adding women for a romantic element at the conclusion, but also as political solutions between nations. However, a totally unique character emerged in her novel *Das Heldenmadchen aus der Vendee* (*The Heroic Maiden of the Vendee*), 1816 when the reader was presented with a beautiful female character who disguised herself as a man so she could join the royalist armies of the Vendee to fight against the Revolution. With a cast of both male and female characters the same beliefs and patriotism coursed through the action. Although it became clear she was not happy in her disguise, the passion for the cause was overwhelming, especially when her love interest Talmont was executed. Politics and the individual quest for peace is interwoven throughout the fabric of all the works by Caroline de la Motte Foque, following the fortunes of certain characters reminiscent of the 'romantic wanderer.' Gender roles are challenged, and the hero/heroine in *The Heroic Maiden of the Vendee* (*Das Heldenmadchen aus der Vendee*) was not the expected male hero but the female Elisabeth Rochefoucault, giving her male readers and critics an unexpected echo of equality and emancipation. Her female readers would have rejoiced.

Sophie Mereau (1770-1806), like Emily died at a young age following what could have been a glorious literary career. She had been a popular figure in the Jena and Weimar circles, which had been a closed area for most women, but her marriage to Karl Mereau, and her natural abilities and willingness to learn allowed her access to the teachings of Goethe, Schiller and Fichte. She was published in their literary journals, and edited the literary journal *Kalathiskos*, Other works she produced included the novel *The Springtime of Sensation* (*Das Bluthenalternbder Empfindung*, 1794) and Amanda und Eduard, a novel in letter form (1803) alongside poems which were produced in two volumes as *Gedichte* (1800-1802). Pressures of society, greed and false hope twists and turns throughout the novel.

Sophie Mereau could also translate English and Italian. With so many abilities it was little wonder she frequently questioned gender roles, looking for equality for women rather than inferiority. Her interest led her to claim she "was not particularly interested in the realist type of novel but in portraying feelings."[16]

Fetting quoted her words which expanded upon her own personal feelings which had some resonance with those of Emily Bronte.

"I found a world inside me that kept me busy, that I wanted to place into reality...I only needed calm from without to shape what lay inside me; Fate did not grant me this calm...my peace is a dream, my joy is the laughter of despair, my harmonies are single discordant notes that resound from distant halls of joy through the wasteland."[17]

A name often overlooked when considering the German female writers was Christiane Benedikt Eugenie Hebenstreit Naubert (1756-1819). She had initially written under the pseudonym Walter von Montbarry, but after being exposed as a woman by K.J. Schutz she used the shortened form of her name; Benedikt Naubert. According to Denis Sweet in *Bitter Healing* "all of Benedikte Nauber's books up to one year before her death were published anonymously. She herself vigorously maintained this anonymity, referring to it as her 'vestal veil,' but this led to 'many of her works being ascribed to other authors, or theirs to her.' The confusion persisted into the twentieth century.[18] Despite the changed response from critics after discovering she was a woman, Naubert went on to write over a variety of fifty novels, novellas and collections of fairy tales (1789-93), bringing recognition from Jacob Grimm who considered Naubert to be, "a very talented and creative female writer."[19] The pure magic and fantasy of the fairy tales were equal to those of the male writers but from an alternate perspective, exploring the position of women in society to create an imaginary ideal world in which knowledge was power.

Shaw C. Jarvis quoted Manfred Gratz who claimed Naubert to be "One of the greatest German popular writers of all times."[20] The fairy tales were examples of the German tradition and influenced by Romanticism, many being translated into English. Denis Sweet stated how "the Romantics, even more than her own generation, came to appreciate Naubert's fairy tales for what Achim von Arnim called their 'fullness' and 'primordiality.' For Arnim, husband of Bettina von Arnim, Naubert's tales were a 'delight in tortured nights."[21] Jarvis in *Shadow of Olympus* claimed that Naubert's novels had influenced both German and English Romanticists from E T A Hoffmann through to Thomas Mann, whilst Walter Scott had admired her historical novels, stating her novels were "excellent romances."[22]

Sophie Albrecht (1757-1840) had been an unconventional writer, following the paths of poet and actress before turning to Gothic-Romantic stories. After her divorce she had cultivated many female friends, and between them they formed quite a network of support for all women writers. A Gothic novel she wrote, and is remembered for, was *The Polite Ghost* (*Das hofliche Gespenst*, 1797), which was re-published five years later under the title of *Ida von Duba*. Full of Gothic machinery, the novel had a central message for young women about having respect for their mothers but also advising against marriages of convenience, whilst set against a background of Hoffmanesque proportions. The story told of how the main character of Katherine was befriended by Ida, without realising that she was a ghost. After Katherine's maid intervenes to discover the identity of the woman she relayed her discovery in full horror, at that point Katherine visited a priest to help her discover

more about the ghost. The priest directed her to a monastery containing an ancient

manuscript, which led to the original story about Ida's past. The image of the monk,

who reported how he became Ida's scribe. alone in his cell, disturbed by the

appearance of Ida's ghost was accompanied by the full force of nature's wrath

conjuring up a supernatural, eerie and uncanny event.

'Storm arose dreadfully, trilled the flags, shook the high trees, struck their anxiously murmuring branches against the windows of my cell, and curled the rustling greenery around the graves at the foot of our walls...Suddenly the doors of my cell flew creakily open; a light like sulphur danced around every object of my chamber; only my little altar stood dark then there was a stirring like anxious groaning coming up to me, then the storm whirled more powerfully- then the sufur flame flickered higher, and Ida, dreadfully enclosed in the blue light, stood in gruesome form before my fixed eyes; woe! woe! she called with a tone that I hope will be spared all fleshly ears-it shook the marrow in my bones: I have been judged restless wandering until I find a woman, more evil and proud than I. Write down, old man! my story, write according to the purest truth! I must tell you to do this; it is the first hour of my humiliation!'[23]

The manuscript told the story of how Ida had persuaded her father to order her

mother, who Ida had previously had declared insane, to perform the lowly service

(usually the job of a servant) of carrying her train at Ida's forthcoming wedding to a

man she was marrying for his wealth and status. Nature, in all her fury raged in a

violent storm, removing Ida's headress which was heavy with jewels. The Gothic

aspects intensified as Ida's body was laid out in her wedding dress, mourners who

were paid to keep watch fled as rumours spread that Ida was still alive. "Poor people

who look at the corpse bemoan the burial of expensive jewels that could mean so

much to them. When her sits up in the casket, the burial is rushed to completion. The coffin is opened once more to dampen wild rumours, but the sight of Ida's decay is so horrible it has the opposite effect."[24]

It was a very powerful Gothic tale, and although we were told how Katherine had travelled abroad and died some years later, we do not get closure in any form for Ida, who we assume will never rest but forever be an eternal wanderer.

The name of Bettina von Arnim (1785-1859) will always be remembered for her adoration of, and letters to Goethe. The granddaughter of Sophie von La Roche, she had been very fortunate to have a large library of books which would have encouraged her early reading experiences, followed by an even larger library of over five thousand books, after her marriage to Achim von Arnim. Bettina had developed a close relationship with the circle of Romanticists at Weimar, thanks to her brother and writer Clemens Brentano. She also had a close friendship with the writer Karoline von Gunderrode (1780-1806) a very deep and tortured soul, expressing the elements of mysticism adopted by the Romantics, as in her poem *Once a Dulcet Life Was Mine* (*Einstens lebt ich susses leben* 1804-5)

'But a deep- down longing held me

Prisoner within myself;

And I felt as if I had been

Wrenched from such sweet flesh at one time,

And were feeling only now

The bleeding wound of pain gone by.

As I turned my flight to where

Lay sweet Earth in blissful slumber

Cradled in the arms of Heaven…'[25]

After three failed relationships, and longing for death, Karoline eventually committed suicide. After Karoline's death Bettina wrote *Die Gunderrode* (1840), which, claimed Baumer, "Despite its innocent appearance as a Romantic correspondence between two young women, contained a good deal of subversive criticism of society and church."[26] Carol Diethe claimed "the early Romantic goals of free and equal conversational exchange, the poeticization of the world, a synthesis of the rational and the emotional, and an understanding of nature without the desire to dominate it, were all better realized in their friendship."[27]

However, it was her letters to Goethe which brought recognition for Bettina, when they were published as *Goethe's Briefwechsel mit einem kinde* (*Goethe's Correspondence with a Child*), in 1835, (four years after the death of her husband), which were described by Carol Diethe as, "a monologue with herself in a quest for the type of self-knowledge which is the goal of the traditional form of but using the highly individualistic method common to Romanticism." [28]

The book was divided into three main sections; Bettina's correspondence with Goethe's mother, followed by her letters to Goethe and his replies, and a third section for Bettina's own diary entries. Throughout the novel there are active exchanges of ideas, reflections and experiences about life and art, music and literature, but the most recurring theme was her adoration of Goethe. According to Wiedenmann, in *Landmarks in German Women's Writing* (2007) the language used by Bettina in

Briefwechsel followed "the pattern of spoken rather than written language, particularly in the first parts and gradually develops into a passionate, erotic language which is full of religious metaphors. This is reminiscent of early Romantic writing such as Friedrich Schlegel's novel *Lucinde*," [29] which was about his love affair with Dorothea Veit; as an early symptom of Romantic rebellion against philistine convention it caused much offence..."[30]

Bettina had claimed that although the book was about Goethe she saw it as a book about love, remarking, "I was not even so especially in love with Goethe; I just needed someone to whom I could vent my thoughts, etc."[31] The book included a letter to her husband in which she attempts to explain her actions,

"precisely that which you criticise, that is the true foundation of everything holy and heavenly, in this exquisite book, here the innocent soul does not have to hide, it can freely pronounce what is its greatest bliss, and it does not need to make the entire public believe that that which is not true. I, an eighteen-year-old child (for that I was a child, as I am today, you know very well), sat on Goethe's lap and immediately, out of blissful peace, fell asleep at his heart and wrote it in drunken joy to Goethe's mother, and that's it; what would there be to lie about? – I want to tell you that the root of the entire trunk is full of magnificent blossoms...without this occurrence, my spirit would not have blossomed through this love." [32]

Although this was recognised as her most important work, Bettina wrote other pieces, relying upon her correspondences and writings. She held literary salons where she could socialize with other women and exchange her views and opinions. These all allowed her to gather material for her work in which she would add her poetry alongside real and invented letters. whilst the "aesthetic theory of the early Romantics was kept alive, far beyond the end of the German Romantic period itself. She incorporated and transgressed early Romantic theories" particularly in her letters and novels, but was still "keen to engage with public discourses regarding social welfare and liberal politics."[33] The result produced was highly original. Bettina had a very sociable and outgoing personality. Diethe concluded that, "Bettina's brand of self-assuredness as a woman unnerved many women as well as men, yet she arguably did more for women's emancipation by her example than all the nineteenth-century tracts on female education put together."[34]

Finally, Johanna Schopenhauer (1766-1838) cannot be ignored, being a central player of the Romantic Movement in Weimar. Her dreams of becoming an artist were thwarted by her parents who considered it as a trade, and arranged for her to marry a much older man when she was only eighteen. Although she had been encouraged to marry Heinrich Florian Schopenhauer, she always insisted that she had not been forced into the marriage.[35]

It was only after his death, an apparent suicide, that she found a new sense of freedom, moving to Weimar in 1806. A gifted linguist, Johanna could speak Polish, English and French in addition to her native German. Her interest in art again resurfaced and she became quite an expert in its theory and application. She cultivated friendships with like-minded people who kept her informed of all happenings in the art world. She later used all she had learned in her novel *Johann van Eyck und seine Nachfolger* (1822), establishing herself as a writer. Goethe had been a frequent house guest, as had other male friends, but it was her relationship with Muller von Gerstenbergk which caused trouble for her. Arthur Schopenhauer, son of Johanna, accused his mother of being unfaithful to the memory of his father. He left home taking his inheritance with him, which he had demanded, leaving Johanna in a poor financial state, particularly so after the Danzig bank collapse in 1819. Johanna got to work writing and published the novel *Gabriele* (1823), followed by Die Tante (1823), Sidonia (1827) and a further novel, Richard Wood (1837), alongside various essays and short stories. Her writings were powerful and emotional, opposing marriage of young girls to older men, particularly in the novel Sidonia. But it was in the novel Gabriele where suffering and death occurred as a result of arranged marriages. Death would have been the sentence for Gabriele if she had refused the marriage as her father was prepared to kill her if she had not accepted her fate. With Gothic images and suggestions of death and suffering, only an escape into the subconscious world of the imagination enabled Gabriele to survive. Johanna did not allow for a happy outcome to the novel, but left questions still to be considered and answered.

Considering the works by female German authors, there are themes similar to those adopted by their male Romantic counterparts, such as love and passion, jealousy and innocence, good against evil, and the overall life against death scenarios, and where the main character is also on a personal journey of self-discovery. However, these themes were not just the 'following on' from the male works, but approached from their individual and personal experiences. It was unfortunate that those articulate and clever writers had to be judged by men. However, they found outlets for their voices through fairy tales (Benedikte Naubert), letters (Bettina von Arnim), poetry (Sophie Mereau) and novels (Annette von Droste-Hulshoff, Caroline de la Motte-Foque and Johanna Schopenhauer). Another unfortunate aspect to the writing life of a woman was that of anti-semitism, experienced by Rahel von Varnhagen, who represented the pain and pressure of double prejudice; being both a woman and Jewish. The female writer Henriette Hertz (1764-1854) had also been persuaded to convert to Christianity. It was not until 1812 that Jewish people had any form of equality, which also varied throughout the country. The stigma of being Jewish led some women to Christianity, which led only to the negative feel of being caught between two worlds.

Letter writing had been not just a form of communication but a way in which to voice opinions, allowing the female voices to be heard. Some of those letters could, and did, create a novel in themselves. Bettina von Arnim's letters to and from Goethe found fame and credibility for her as a writer. Where the female writer excelled over the male was in the use of emotions. The women who wrote in Germany were many and varied, although the majority of those were from aristocratic families, or, had been fortunate to have received education, the type of whichcould cause barriers to be raised against them forcing them into one or other genre. But most of all, women learned by their instincts; through nature and their own imaginations, desires and dreams, asserting their femininity and frustrations.

Familiar landscapes became places of spiritual and creative inspiration, offering freedom and self-discovery, the essence of which was captured by Bettina von Arnim,

> Upon this hill, I look upon my
>
> World.
>
> And if I were to gain a glimpse
>
> Of paradise
>
> I would long to return
>
> To the meadows here
>
> Where your lowered roof
>
> Reveals itself to me
>
> For, that, alone, defines my
>
> World.[36]

It is only in recent years that the Romantic German female creative endeavours have finally found recognition. The barrier to women's publishing success in Germany was a reflection of that faced by the women writers in England; male domination. Their determination, however, to compete in a man's world did not stop them from picking up their pens in a bid to be heard. It seemed as though Romanticism had reached out far and wide, encompassing aspiring artists of all genres and abilities.

CHAPTER SIX: Wuthering Heights

During the late eighteenth century Europe began to see many changes following

previous disastrous wars and political doctrines, particularly the French Revolution.

With the new industrial age came new ideas, not only in science and technology but

also by the intellectual and artistic movements. Artists of all genres were free from

old classical constraints to explore and develop their own distinctive styles. It was not

long before England found itself with many new poets and writers. The novel form,

under the influence of Romanticism began to flourish and as Chris Baldick

commented, it became the 'most important literary genre of the modern age,

superseding the 'epic,' the 'romance,' and other narrative forms.' He pointed out that "the novel tended towards realism [Jane Austen and George Eliot] in a recognisable social world, [had] at least one character, and preferably several characters shown in processes of change and social relationships, a plot and narrated events."[1]

Peck and Coyle defined the novel as having 'many ingredients,' and the impressions of certain characteristics [which could] sway our opinions, allowing us to relate to them in some way. They identified the 'plot' as being the cause and effect mechanism, being the selected version of events as presented to the reader or audience in a certain order or duration.

Chris Baldick cited the philosophy of Aristotle,"who saw plot as more than just the arrangements of incidents [but] the most important function in a drama as a governing principle of development and coherence to which other elements (including character) must be subordinated. He insisted that a plot should have a beginning, a middle and an end, and that its events should form a coherent whole." Baldick concluded that "most plots will trace some process of change in which characters are caught up in a developing conflict that is finally resolved."[2]

The role of the narrator in the novel occupies a unique position in that he can tell the story in first-person narrative, which gives a more direct insight into a character, his personality and motives. The narrator can also be omniscient; telling the story without the reader being aware of him. Occasionally the reader will be presented with unreliable narrators who can be characters in the story, or can give comments according to their own opinions. In *Wuthering Heights* there are two narrators; Nelly Dean and Mr. Lockwood, who narrated the story from the fringes of the novel, indicating that events were puzzling, intriguing and disturbing. From the variety of definitions about the novel it is not so easy to place *Wuthering Heights*, although it can appear to be a 'realist' novel, in that it depicted real Yorkshire people and dialogue, it also contained a wealth of Romanticism and Gothic aspects in its haunting narrative. Many of the aspects employed by EmilyBronte in her writing compared strikingly with the German novelle.

In the novel *Wuthering Heights* the emotions are explored over the full spectrum, often verging on the fantastic, making it a most powerful and haunting novel. Gareth Lloyd Evans indicated, like many critics before him, that to explore Emily's imagination "must be a journey into what is probably mostly unknowable or, at least inexpressible, and remote from familiar haunts of biography."[3]

Wuthering Heights was firmly set in its time and place; early nineteenth century rural Yorkshire, having been faithful to the Yorkshire dialect, and set in a vast cold, remote and forbidding landscape of the Yorkshire moors. Further reading takes the reader into another world completely with hostile characters, satanic imagery, longing for death, ghosts and hauntings. James Senior stated, *Wuthering Heights* "was the most passionate, intense and weird of all stories I have read."[4] Despite retaining its appeal over the years, Wemyss Reid claimed the novel [after initial publication] had "never electrified London society, though in 1850 it found a warm champion in Sydney Dobell, who had claimed 'Not a subordinate place or person in this novel but bears more or less the stamp of high genius.' However, by 1877 it was practically unread [and] a book from which readers turned away with something like a shudder."[5] Charles Simpson found *Wuthering Heights* to be strangely original,' bearing "resemblance to some of those irregular German tales in which the writers, giving the reins to their fancy, represent personages as swayed and impelled to evil by supernatural forces"[6]

Winifred Gerin, quoting from a review in Douglas Jerrold's *Weekly*, stated that *Wuthering Heights* "readers would be shocked, disgusted, almost sickened by details of cruelty, inhumanity and the most diabolical hate and vengeance, but recommended it to those 'who love novelty...for we can promise them that they have never read anything like it before."[7]

The isolation of the book's setting, its unusual characters, two main narrators; Nelly and Mr. Lockwood, use of Yorkshire dialect in bleak circumstances, and curtness of manners, would have appeared alien to city readers, despite the surge earlier in the century for Gothic fiction. During the reign of Queen Victoria the novels regained their popularity and have retained that popularity ever since, particularly by academic writers and critics who have used all manner of tools at their disposal to deconstruct many aspects of the novels by the Bronte sisters, especially *Wuthering Heights*.

Charlotte Bronte had claimed "with regard to *Wuthering Heights*...it is moorish and wild, and knotty as a root of heather."[8] In her *Preface to the New Edition of Wuthering Heights* (1850) Charlotte recognised that readers from other areas, not familiar with Yorkshire and its setting for *Wuthering Heights* must have found little of interest, "the language, the manners, the very dwellings and household customs of the scattered inhabitants of those districts, must be to some readers in a great measure unintelligible, and – where intelligible – repulsive and that they would not know what to make of the rough, strong utterances, the harshly manifested passions, the unbridled aversions and headlong partialities of unlettered moorland hinds and rugged moorland squires."[9] About the quality of *Wuthering Heights*, Charlotte added that it was "rustic all through…of natural scenery Emily's descriptions were what they should be, and all they should be."[10]

The Eclectic Review was one such area of negativity, commenting upon the bleakness of the surroundings and general atmosphere of the novel finding the characters to be "a company we never saw grouped before; and we hope never to meet with its like again," adding that "Heathcliff is a perfect monster, more demon than human. Hindley Earnshaw is a besotted fool, for whom we scarce feel pity; while his son Hareton is at once ignorant and brutish, until, as by the wand of an enchanter, he takes polish in the last scene of the tale, and retires a docile and apt scholar." About the two Catherines' The *Review* stated they were "absurdly unnatural in the leading incidents of their life. Isabella Linton is one of the silliest and most credulous girl that fancy ever painted; and the enduring affection and tenderness of her brother Edgar are so exhibited as to produce the impression of a feeble rather than of a virtuous character." The *Review's* other negative comments found the plot to be "sadly wanting in probability," whilst its characters were "unattractive, devoid of truthfulness, and not in harmony with the actual world, have little power to move our sympathies than the romances of the Middle Ages, or the ghost stories which made our granddames tremble."[11]

Charlotte defended such criticisms, stating that the "true source of the novel is the actual wild way of life of the peasants of Yorkshire. The novel is sociologically accurate. Emily is merely the innocent transcriber of fact; she knew them; knew their ways, their language, their family histories; she could hear of them with interest, and talk of them with detail, minute, graphic, and accurate…Her imagination, which was a spirit more sombre than sunny, more powerful than sportive, found in such traits material whence it wrought creations like Heathcliff, like Earnshaw, like Catherine. Having formed these beings she did not know what she had done.[12] Emily had, in effect acted as a medium through which something or someone else spoke.

Charlotte had also commented upon Emily's often, 'strange' behaviour and how she "was not a person to demonstrate character, nor one, on the recesses of whose mind and feelings, even those nearest and dearest to her could, with impunity, intrude unlicensed."[13] Lucaster Miller referred to Emily's final illness in which Charlotte needed to placate Emily further, and how 'it was useless to question her- you get no answers – it is still more useless to recommend remedies – they are never adopted…you must look on, and see her do what she is unfit to do, and not dare say a word." Yet, Miller concluded,' in the letters leading up to Emily's death Charlotte gives us frustratingly little access to her sister's motives or desires, what she calls Emily's peculiar reserve of character shuts her out."[14]

Evidence had shown how at both Roe Head and Brussels, Charlotte had attempted to broaden Emily's experiences, but both had resulted with her taking

Emily home. Charlotte had commented how 'I felt in my heart she would die if she did not go home, and with this conviction obtained her recall.' Charlotte had reflected upon how "Emily did not care what people thought. Her refusal to behave with conventional ladylike manners – like her perverse but determined choice of unfashionable clothes – caused Charlotte agonies of embarrassment," plus, how she "was most reluctant to imitate the style of other writers' as instructed by Constantine Heger at his Brussel's school."[15]

On a more positive note, Charles Simpson defined Emily's personality at twenty seven as an "extremely intellectual young woman. Allied to the poetical side of her nature was a power of intellect that had impressed Monsieur Heger in Brussels. He considered that, had she been a man, she would have been a great explorer or navigator; as a writer, he thought she might have been a great historian. The unsophisticated side of her (as she appeared to others) was partly the result of her absolute independence of thought. She could not think in current channels, or adopt the conventional mode of approaching any problem whatever. She kept her mind completely clear from submission to thoughts not her own, or from any domination in any way by the mind of another. Yet she had nothing of the arrogance of intellect with which her independence of thought might be confused. There was about her the humility of the true mystic, a quality inseparable from mysticism, but it was a humility that bowed to no man on earth."[16] May Sinclaire agreed, stating, "you may call her what you will – Pagan, pantheist, transcendentalist, mystic, and worshipper of earth, she slips through all your formulas. She reveals a point of view *above* good and evil."[17] It was an opinion also shared by Charles Morgan, who added "we are on dangerous ground – dangerous because no theory about Emily Brontë's inner life is capable of final proof, doubly dangerous because in many minds, the 's are an obsession which, while it lasts, attaches to them the privileges and penalties of Caesar's wife."[18]

Ellen Nussey, a close family friend of the 's recalled how Emily Bronte" did not talk so much as the rest of the party, but her wonderful eyes, brilliant and unfathomable as the pool at the foot of a waterfall, but radiant also with a wealth of tenderness and warmth, show how her soul is expanding under the influences of the scene (countryside)…she utters at times a deep guttural sound which those who know her best interpret as the language of a joy too deep for articulate expression."[19]

The comments made about the personality of Emily Bronte seem to mark her out as truly original, unique person, but there was a suggestion made by Ellen Nussey that Emily could display rather strange language and behaviour. She did not like to communicate with people outside of the family, being only happy when she was in familiar surroundings. Charlotte Brontë's own struggles to protect the reputation of her sister also came under the spotlight. Compiling such evidence would point to Emily suffering from what we know in modern times, to be recognised as Asperger's syndrome. It would certainly seem to fit all descriptions of her lack of eye contact, social isolation and odd behaviour, despite her intelligence. A. Mary F. Robinson stated "In those days they could not tell that the defect was incurable, a congenital infirmity of nature."[20]

The writer T. S. Eliot had said of Emily that, "she was talking to herself all the time; talking of things which were intimate to her but jealously guarded from the whole world. And the privacy of her speech was the more heightened in that her self-communication was not of a cool and rational order. It was passionate utterance; passionate confession; but confession to nobody save her own self."[21]

By analysing the novel form of *Wuthering Heights*; its construction, sequencing and timelessness, alongside characters who seem to communicate in 'atmospheres,' or by mood and facial expression, it was a novel grounded in the reality of Emily 's own existence, and so a product fused by artistic and mental 'uniqueness.' Many incidents from her own life can be found in *Wuthering Heights*, such as when Catherine is bitten by the bulldog and does not scream, shout or display anguish and hurt. In her own life Emily, also, was bitten by a possible rabied dog, but she did not panic, simply cauterized the wound with a hot iron herself. She had also put out a fire with her bare hands when her brother Branwell, in a drunken stupor set fire to the blanket he was wrapped in. Further, in the novel, (chapter seventeen) Isabella had a knife thrown at her which lodged in her neck. She commented how, "it struck me beneath my ear, and stopped the sentence I was uttering; but pulling it out, I sprang to the door, and delivered another which I hope went a little deeper than his missile." [22] The shock and pain must have been great, but once again, Isabella does not give a reaction which would be considered 'normal,' except as retaliation. Other violent episodes included Nelly having a knife pushed into her mouth, to which she claimed, "he [Hindley] held the knife in his hand, and pushed its point between my teeth; but, for my part, I was never much afraid of his vagaries. I spat it out, and affirmed it tasted detestably – I would not take it on any account."[23] also the beating of Heathcliff, by Hindley and Joseph, which became the catalyst for his revenge.

A.Mary F. Robinson commented that "this is the plot; but to make a character speak, act, rave, love, live, die through a whole lifetime of events, even as the readers feel convinced he must have acted, must have lived and died, this demands at least so much experience of a somewhat similar nature as may serve for a base to one's imagination, a reserve of certainty and reassurance on which to draw in times of perplexity and doubt."[24]

E.M. Forster's discussion about *Wuthering Heights* in *Aspects of the Novel* also questioned "why did she deliberately introduce muddle, chaos, tempest?" He continued to speculate that "always in the back of my mind, there lurks a reservation about this prophetic stuff, a reservation which some will make more strongly while others will not make it at all."[25] The psychological aspects of Emily 's personality would require further research to be undertaken by an author qualified in that field of expertise. However, A. Stuart Daley had compiled an excellent chronology of events for *Wuthering Heights*, dated from 1757 through to 1803, in which all the major events of the action are recorded.[26]

The Yorkshire moors meant that people were remote, but also close-knit, often inter-related. The same scenario could be seen in *Wuthering Heights*, with the only travel being to Liverpool, from where Mr. Earnshaw returned with the young Heathcliff. That incident of the novel had been a source of intrigue for critics of the novel who asked if Mr. Earnshaw *did* actually walk one hundred and twenty miles in three days? This aspect of the novel has been speculated upon over the years by various critics; where exactly did Mr. Earnshaw encounter Heathcliff and what was his background? The reader is simply told that efforts were made to locate his family, but without success. Mr. Earnshaw described Heathcliff as a "gift from God," but "they entirely refused to have it in bed with them, or even in their rooms…"[27]

The Irish immigration problem during the 1840's was reported in the *Illustrated London News*, who wrote about the hundreds of children who were "like starving scarecrows with a few rags on them and an animal growth of black hair [which] almost obscured their features."[28] In the preface to the 1850 edition of *Wuthering Heights* Charlotte described Heathcliff as "a child neither of Lascar nor gipsy, but a man's shape animated by demon life – a ghoul – an Afreet!"[29]

Many Irish families arrived on Liverpool docks daily, often becoming displaced, leaving many children alone, vulnerable and starving. People in England were aware of their plight, and the Church in Haworth was no exception. The Reverend informed his congregation and collected donations to help. The family would have felt a connection and empathy for the immigrants, as the family also had their origins in Ireland. In *Wuthering Heights*, Mr. Earnshaw saw his way of contributing to the cause by adopting the young Heathcliff, who was quite unrecognisable by the family because of his dirty appearance, and they referred to him initially as 'it.' He was named Heathcliff by Mr. Earnshaw, after the late son of the Earnshaws who had died in childbirth. "The unfolding immigration drama in the country at the time would have given Emily the information she needed to explain the appearance of Heathcliff in her novel. She had also learned a great deal about Liverpool from her brother Branwell, who had made the journey to Liverpool in a barge with his friend Hartley Merrall, as suggested by Daphne Du Maurier,[30]and where "the sea and the docks on Merseyside must have proved a great attraction."[31] Upon returning home, Branwell entertained the family with tales about Liverpool, insisting they must all visit, which unfortunately it was one journey they never managed.

Emily's *Wuthering Heights* at time seems an alien and hostile place but like her own inner world, both flashes of fantasy and reality were ingrained throughout. Emotions exhibited in the poetry of Emily emerged throughout the novel, with the spirit of the moors, adored by Emily. *Wuthering Heights* also gave an odd, cold and detached view of romantic love, which may have been the impression she was given, having witnessed the traumatic effects the emotion of love had upon Charlotte, following her doomed passion for Ms. Heger, as well as Branwell's fated lost love Lydia Robinson. With so much depression and despair around her Emily could not have avoided being affected. Du Maurier commented, "What a blessed relief it must have been for Emily to stride away over the moors with her dog, and put aside, if only for an hour on a winter's afternoon, the memory of her brother humped on his bed thinking of his Lydia, and her sister couched on the dining-room sofa brooding on her professor."[32] It perhaps also explained why "she nowhere shows any proper abhorrence of the fiendish and vindictive Heathcliff." But, as Robinson pointed out, "she submits as patiently to his swarthy soul and savage instincts as to his swarthy skin and 'gibberish' that nobody could understand."[33]

Wuthering Heights portrayed a cyclical process of both creation and destruction. It was the duality ingrained in the novel which was most apparent, from the cold remote, masculine and forbidding *Wuthering Heights* to the warm, feminine family seat of Thrushcross Grange, home to the Linton family. The novel however, was male dominated because of the strong presence of Heathcliff, who had an effect upon everyone around him. Even Lockwood fell under the atmosphere of violence and the supernatural, dreaming about a child ghost tapping on his window, to which he pulled "its wrist on the broken pane, and rubbed it to and fro till the blood ran down and soaked the bedclothes,"[34] the image of blood giving a very Gothic feel.

On the feminine side of the action in the novel there are the two Catherines' and Isabella, with Nelly giving an ongoing commentary. As children, Heathcliff was the soul-mate of Catherine, but during her stay at Thrushcross Grange, after being bitten by the dog Skulker, she saw that her life could be very different, seeing herself as "the greatest woman of the neighbourhood."[35] She wanted both *Wuthering Heights* and Thrushcross Grange, being unable to make her mind up between marriage to Edgar Linton, and her long standing passion for Heathcliff. An aspect of fate and destiny took place when Heathcliff learned of Catherine's choice, realising he could never have Catherine until he reached a higher social standing. The novel then descended into the "ravings and ragings of the villain against the man whose life stands between him and the woman he loves."[36] Heathcliff's ravings and the words he chose would have resonated with those uttered by Branwell, which Emily would have witnessed as he agonised about his lost love, Mrs Robinson, as he claimed, "My own life without her will be hell. What can the so-called love of her wretched sickly husband be to her compared with mine."[37] In *Wuthering Heights* Heathcliff also raved about Catherine, and he claimed, "Two words would comprehend my future-death and hell; existence after losing her would be hell. Yet, I was a fool to fancy for a moment that she valued Edgar Linton's attachment more than mine. If he loved with all the powers of his puny being, he couldn't love in eighty years as much as I could in a day."[38] Du Maurier concluded that "Hindley Earnshaw and the carving knife, Heathcliff dashing his head against a tree and howling like a savage beast, were all part of Branwell's infernal world."[39] Emily's own world was disturbed by those reckless incidents caused by her brother's irresponsible and unpredictable nature. As Mary F. Robinson pointed out, 1846, the year Emily was writing *Wuthering Heights*, must have been anxious and troubled and the heaviest and dreariest days of her life; it was during their weary course that she at last perceived how utterly hopeless, how insensible to god, must be to the remaining life of her brother."[40]

We are made aware of a three year time span accounting for the disappearance of Heathcliff, returning to find Catherine has married and given birth to the younger Catherine, but after a passionate encounter with Heathcliff she succumbed to madness and finally died. Catherine's spirit hovered over the rest of the novel, with Heathcliff unable to escape from her spectre, becoming quite mad as he called out to her, "Catherine Earnshaw, may you not rest as long as I am living. You said I killed you – haunt me then…I know that ghosts have wandered the earth. Be with me always – take any for – drive me mad."[41] He made the conscious decision finally to commit suicide so he could join his beloved Catherine in death. As though knowing about his plot to disinherit Hareton and the young Catherine, the ghost of the older Catherine appeared to haunt Heathcliff, putting extra pressure on him, confirmed by his comment to Nelly, "[there is] a strange change approaching – I am in its shadow at present."[42]

All life and death can be found in the novel of *Wuthering Heights*. It contained features and elements found in the works of the German Romantics, with its dark, brooding hero Heathcliff and his "surreptitious visits to her (Catherine's) grave, his midnight walking and sharp teeth [to] invoke vampiric associations,"[43] tragedy of lost love, madness and the Gothic supernatural, all taken to extremes within the backdrop of an ever-changing transcendental nature into a brand new world. The conclusion to *Wuthering Heights* was one of relief, as the all-pervading tensions and pressures of fear and madness receded with the unexpected death of Heathcliff. As the winter of discontent gave way to spring, it also allowed a new beginning for the young Hareton and the second Catherine to finally have much needed peace in their lives. However, the same could not be said for Catherine and Heathcliff who, claimed locals, had see their ghosts. Heathcliff had been buried in unconsecrated ground next to Catherine, following the Georgian Pagan tradition in which suicides would not be allowed the hope of Christian resurrection. Prior to the late eighteenth century anyone committing suicide was "impaled in their graves with a stake through their hearts in a rite of Pagan origin; the stake came to be seen as preventing the resurrection of suicides on Judgement day. The suicide's corpse was buried at a crossroads in the hope that the sign of the cross would drive off the devil. Christians were buried in graves facing east-west so that they could rise up to face God on Judgement Day; they were interred among other members of their family to emphasise the community of the dead."[44] It was not until 1882 that the law permitted suicides to be buried in daytime hours, when previously they had to be buried between nine o'clock and midnight. In *Wuthering Heights*, following the earlier death of Hindley Earnshaw, Heathcliff had raved "that fool's body should be buried at the crossroads, without ceremony of any kind for he had spent the night in drinking himself to death deliberately." Though it would be crude to treat the relationship between Heathcliff and Catherine as that of a vampire and his prey, their passionate, destructive involvement, his emotions during his surreptitious visits to her grave, his midnight walking and sharp teeth invoke vampiric associations. The anomalies surrounding his death connote the same set of beliefs surrounding vampires and self-murder. "[45] 'Is he a ghoul or a vampire? Mused his servant Nelly Dean."[46]

Charlotte commented that the scenes of horror in *Wuthering Heights* 'banished sleep by night and disturbed mental peace by day,'[47] then the identification of Branwell with Hindley Earnshaw was [also] very possible. *Wuthering Heights* was a mixture of styles as well as influences which has made it a unique literary product, but also one in which location played a major role, as it also did in many of the

German prose works. Mary Sinclair commented about *Wuthering Heights*, "this book stands alone, absolutely self-begotten and self-born. It belongs to no school; it follows no tendency; you cannot put it into any category. It is not 'Realism,' it is not 'Romance,' any more than *Jane Eyre*; and if any other master's method, De Maupassant's or Turgeniev's, is to be the test, it will not stand it. There is nothing in it you can seize and name."[48]

Romer Wilson claimed that E.T.A Hoffman's *The Entail* was the inspiration and catalyst for *Wuthering Heights*. Romer Wilson stated that Emily was probably trying to emulate Hoffmann, such as her admiration was for the German writer. It does seem probable that some of the ideas used by Hoffmann may have found their way into the imagination of Emily Bronte; landscape, atmosphere, murder, hauntings, characters, and narrators, which were also the staple ingredients of most Gothic novels.

"Hoffmann told the story of a visit to a lonely castle on a deserted moor. After an historic preamble, for which Emily substituted the past history of the reader's friend, Mr. Lockwood, for two men, the narrator and he who is to tell the real story within this story, visit an old castle at night in a snow storm where an old servant of extraordinary figure lets them in after considerable ado. The younger of these men, the narrator, spends his first evening reading a gruesome volume, Schiller's *Ghost-Seer*, which reading is followed by a nightmare in which he hears 'sighing and groaning [in which] "lay an expression of the most inconsolable misery...there came a scraping, and louder, deeper sighs, as if emitted in the dread of death, and there came from behind the new wall."[49] moaning at intervals, and in this sighing and moaning there was expressed the deepest trouble, the most hopeless grief, that a human being can know.' These sounds are accompanied by a scratching on the wall as of some imprisoned animal. He stated that the story could be summarized as "a tale of passionate love and bitter feelings of a usurper and an orphan heir. The R- family history is connected with two houses, one this gloomy castle, and one a fine estate in Courland"[50] In *Wuthering Heights* the tension also took place between the two houses of the Lintons and Wuthering Heights. An incident in *Wuthering Heights* in which Lockwood cuts his hands on the broken glass had its likeness in *The Entail* in which Daniel "began to scratch at the wall with his hands, so that blood was soon spurting out from under his nails, while groaning as if tormented by the pangs of death,"[51]

The relaying of the history behind the hauntings was similar to that between Lockwood and Nelly Dean, accompanied by the uncle crying out to the ghost of Daniel,[52] as Heathcliff did to the ghost of Catherine. He continued to add that the orphan heir of the gloomy castle married the heiress of Courland. The evidence points to a connection and direct influence to the plot of Wuthering Heights, placing its location on the bleak Yorkshire moors. The characters also bore strong resemblance to those in *Wuthering Heights*; Joseph being the replacement for Daniel the old estate lawyer, Catherine Earnshaw as Seraphina, and that "Heathcliff is cousin in darkness of the soul of the R- family, a soul that had dealings with the devil and the black arts."[53] Just as Heathcliff has an obsessional love for Catherine, Hoffmann's character of Theodore had been obsessed with the Baroness.

The landscape too found its way from the pages of Hoffmann as "the dark and "mournful child who found himself cast upon a moor among strangers," and who finally ended his own life, as Heathcliff did, with those infamous lines, "his unrepentant ghost walked hand-in-hand with his soul upon the moor."[54]

Nature was important in Hoffmann's tale, as it was in *Wuthering Heights*, the cold, harsh backgrounds of snow and wind adding to the Gothic atmosphere. "They say that nature represents the cycle of human life symbolically in the changing seasons...the spring mists fall, the summer haze shimmers, and only in the clear ether of autumn can the distant landscape be seen clearly before the world is immersed in the night of winter."[55] The conclusions to both novels have their similarities in that Heathcliff's plans to stop his son and the second Catherine from inheriting *Wuthering Heights* are thwarted, whilst Hoffmann's castle fell into the hands of the state.

Death was an inevitable element to the Gothic poet and writer, whether by murder, illness or otherwise, and always accompanied by the certainty of life continuing after death. That belief led Emily Bronte to question such an assumption through her poems and novel. She was to discover the truth earlier that she should have, as Emily appeared to have taken her own life, refusing food, drink and a doctor until the last moments of her life, as though in full knowledge of what she was doing. Romer Wilson pointed out how "she persisted in dying, and dying alone, by night, and by day is terribly clear...refused everything until almost the last minute of her life [when] she whispered, 'if you will send for a doctor, I will see him now!'" [56]

Whatever the view of the critic, *Wuthering Heights* emerged from all the influences around Emily Bronte; her strong religious beliefs, her physical surroundings of the church and its graveyard, which must have been food for the imaginations of the young children growing up. Education had been an important element too, with frequent trips to the library at the Mechanic's Institute, and the reading of both English and German authors. We already know from Mrs. Gaskell that Emily tried to learn the German language, and that she and Charlotte became quite proficient in French. Later, when Patrick 's eyes began to fail, Emily would sit and read to him, usually works by Goethe, Schiller, Hoffmann and others whose popularity was high in England during those first few decades of the nineteenth century But it was the surrounding moorlands, with its many faceted outlook as the seasons changed which had a profound effect upon the moods of the inhabitants, especially Emily who felt at one with the natural world.

CONCLUSION

Throughout this study I have attempted to show how German Romanticism influenced Emily Bronte, who was recognised by Dobree as being "the greatest poetess England has produced, with possible exception of Christina Rossetti; but one feels that if she had lived, she would have held first place unrivalled."[1] The analysis aimed at exploring the literary world of Emily Bronte, its religious and spiritual construction, the term 'mystic' and the overall influences of the German Romantic Movement. The Romantic devices and Gothic elements in her work produced an interesting and convincing image of an unconventional and highly individual poet.

The broader cultural background of Emily; her Yorkshire roots and surroundings, particularly the moors which were so instrumental in her work, provided a landscape from which she could draw upon all her reserves. The moors were vital to her growth and well- being, and essential to her existence. When she had been far away from them she suffered. Charlotte's notes about Emily confirmed that; "If her spirit was more sombre than sunny, the explanation is to be found in the mind of the artist, as a painter may see dark and subdued tones a beauty that others find in bright harmonies. Such are born, and no contact with a world outside their own can change them."[2]

The same comments could also have been applied to the German Romantic poets, who relied upon nature and the natural world to establish, define and create numerous worlds in their works. With imaginative expression and drawing their themes and subjects from nature made them like 'landscape painters in words,' an expression used by Charles Simpson to describe Emily Bronte. A closer examination of her poetry revealed a wild landscape, where night or day became symbolic of the spiritual world. As with the German Romantics, who also responded to morning, for example, in a hopeful way with the additional natural sounds of bird song, sunshine and a general mood of apprehension and expectancy, while the day-time hours developed an air of oppressiveness as life took on a wistful and melancholy feel. But, as the study has shown it was the night which created a background for the Romantic poets, and on which Emily Bronte concentrated much of her poetry. The night for Novalis brought the poet nearer to God. For Emily Bronte it brought dreams, visions and a divine longing. It also provided darkness and comfort, blocking out cold forbidding reality. It was those very obvious symbolic references that aligned Emily Bronte with the German romantic poets; all had their own similar pattern of thought and style, despite their different languages and range of approaches. Mark Kipperman stated, "In their different ways, the Romantic poets explored the ground of the subject-object relation, the nature and possibility of true interchange. The activity establishing, defining and creating this relation was the imagination."[3]

The imagination referred was charged with a supernatural element that elevated the poet from any mundane existence to a higher spiritual form, which became termed 'transcendental,' where the focus of the mind sought to create on "its own terms a world of evolving spiritual revelation or significance."[4] Emily Bronte had been called a mystic because of this ability to transcend reality. She had this in common with Novalis, who was also known as a mystic. Caroline Spurgeon, in her book *Mysticism in English Literature*, stated, "the mystic bases his belief, not on revelation, logic, reason, or demonstrated facts, but on 'feeling,' or intuitive inner knowledge."[5] Her book classes Emily Bronte within the remit of the philosophical mystics, alongside the seventeenth century poet Thomas Traherne, who claimed, "you never enjoy the world aright, till the Sea itself floweth in your veins, till you are clothed with the heavens, and crowned with the stars…Till you can sing and rejoice and delight in God, as misers do in gold, and Kings in sceptres, you never enjoy the world…The world is a mirror of infinite beauty, yet no man sees it. It is a temple of majesty, yet no man regards it. It is a region of Light and Peace, did not men disquiet it, It is the Paradise of God…It is the place of Angels and the Gate of Heaven."[6]

Emily Bronte was, according to Spurgeon, "an unusual type of mystic. Indeed, she is one of the most strange and baffling figures in our literature." About her poems, she considered them to be "strong and free and certain, hampered by no dogma, weighted by no explanation, but containing – in the simplest language – the record of the experience and the vision of a soul."[7] Defining the mysticism of Emily Bronte, she found two forms, firstly her "unerring appreciation of values, of the illusory quality of material things, even of the nature she so loved, together with the certain vision of the one Reality behind all forms, This, and her descriptions of ecstasy, of the all-sufficing experience, mark her out as being among those who have seen, and who know."[8] In a psychic study of Emily Bronte, Millicint Collard claimed, Emily had "a strong psychic nature, contact with the dead and second sight."[9] Although it was pure conjecture based upon random evidence, such as there being thirty four chapters to *Wuthering Heights*, the age of Jesus when he died, and other vague observations, it did start Bronte critics reading more closely to find out if there was any truth in the assertions. Plus, even Charlotte was perplexed by Emily's odd behaviour and trance-like state, as Ann asked why Emily had an empty look in her eyes, to which Charlotte had replied, "I don't quite know…While it possesses her she is no longer mine."[10] Apparently, Emily was thought to be seeing a ghost whenever it happened!

Schelling's theoretical idealism recognised such a condition, stating, "In all of us there dwells a mysterious and wonderful power to withdraw ourselves from the changes of time into our innermost self, freed from all that comes to us from without, and to intuit the eternal in us under the form of immutability…in this moment of intuition time and duration vanish for us, we are no longer in time, but time is in us – or, rather, not time, but pure, absolute eternity."[11] The quest for eternity was an ongoing endeavour for Emily Bronte in her lifetime, but if we were to believe the claim of psychic clergyman, Charles L. Tweedale, who attempted to contact Emily in a séance, she replied, telling him to "walk round my music stool and play on my piano and say Emily Bronte, I love you...then upstairs you must go/To see my dress, and ask that you/May always be dressed in blue."[12] Clearly Emily had found her ever-after if we are to believe his claim.

Novalis and the German Romantic poets held the same longings in their quest for a heightened spiritual world, and a divine presence in nature. Charles Simpson stated that "A knowledge of mysticism is necessary to appreciate the development of Emily's poetical genius."[13] According to Novalis it was a 'romanticizing' of the world. "The world must be romanticized, only thus will we discover its original meaning…if I give a higher meaning to the everyday, a mysterious aspect to the ordinary, the dignity of the unfamiliar to the familiar, the appearance of infinity to the finite, then I am romanticizing it…we recognise ourselves in innumerable unsuspecting guises and meet ourselves constantly in the natural world (in stone and flowers)."[14]

The world of Gondal, examined in Chapter two had also not escaped the German romantic influence. Nature, man, God, visions and the subconscious all emerged from the imaginary poetry of Emily Bronte. It has been difficult to deny the European Romantic and Gothic influences even in Gondal. As Lyn Pykett pointed out, "Emily's powerful women offer the female versions of the Romantic exile, that outcast, outlawed, or otherwise isolated figure, the lone bearer of the truth who rejects or rebels against the society from which she has been exiled."[15] The writing of the Gondal poetry allowed Emily to distance herself from life, and to experiment with the Gothic forms of death and destruction, Heaven and Hell scenarios, in imaginary and powerfully charged atmospheres and landscapes. Her vivid descriptions of battle-scenes and heroic deaths may have, at one time, provided an exciting interlude in her life, but the underlying structure admits more than what its characters say, as Emily's own subconscious thoughts surface, "Oh, for the day, when I shall rest/ And never suffer more."[16] T.S Elliot said of Emily, "She was talking to herself nearly all the time; talking of things which were intimate to her but jealously guarded from the whole world. And the privacy of her speech was the more heightened in that her self-communion was not of a cool and rational order. It was passionate utterance; passionate confession; but confession to nobody save her own self."[17]

The poetry of Emily Bronte was passionate and sincere. Her solitary walks on the moors allowed her to be the Romantic wanderer, to be at one with nature and share its secrets. Her poems represented the changing face of nature, its extremities and complexities, where she could meditate upon her own emotional instincts. Those were the moments she shared with the German Romantics. The influences on Emily have been many and varied, but always return to the European affinity. *Blackwood's* and *Frazer's* had triggered a taste for German literature during those early decades of the nineteenth century; something that was endorsed by Thomas Carlyle, Sir Walter Scott, Coleridge, Madame de Staël and other cultural commentators. The work of German writers such as E. T. A Hoffmann, and poets such Goethe and Schiller, had dominated the English literary scene, displaying the new aesthetic ground of German Romantic literature. It was interesting to note that *Blackwood's Edinburgh Magazine* often published Schiller's poems and ballads in their original fragment form. In the April 1843 magazine Schiller's *Expectation and Fulfilment* (two-line poem), *Value and Worth* (Two-line poem) and *To the Proselyte Maker* (four- line poem) were published.[18] The 'fragment' poem had become a feature of the Romantic Movement. According to Glyn Tegai Hughes, Novalis "Remains the vivid creator (with Friedrich Schlegel) of a new, revolutionary, and still only partly accepted form."[19] The "Fragmentary form has seen to represent a characteristic attitude, but in Novalis's case, the influence of Friedrich Schlegel's enthusiasm may have been decisive. Both see the fragment as being something more open-ended than the rather sententious aphorisms of the eighteenth century. Novalis's fragments in particular are more confessional, more speculative, depth-charges rather than constructs. In a letter to Schelling he calls his own attempts 'fragments of the continuing dialogue with myself-cuttings [in a horticultural sense.][20] Hughes concluded that the "Creativity and novelty of his language make the fragments the most breathtaking of all the products of German Romanticism."[21]

Amongst the poems of Emily Bronte can be found similar fragments, which had been thought by biographers to be a part of other poems, or merely drafts, but arguably the German Romantic influence could be seen to be responsible, as Emily experimented with the new form. The fragment "There are two trees in a lonely field/All waving solemnly,"[22] painted a picture in words of a complete Romantic-Gothic landscape, reflecting the melancholy emotions of the poet. In just a few lines Emily Bronte captured the essence of the scene. Again, in the two-line fragment, "What is that smoke that ever still/Comes rolling down that dark brown hill,"[23] where the image was captured of descending fog on the moors and hillsides. Sounds too were incorporated into her fragments to establish related atmosphere, "Coldly, bleakly drearily/Evening died on Elbës shore/Winds were in the cloudy sky/ sighing mourning ever more."[24] The rhythm of the sea and the wind were captured in the Gondal fragment where "From the intensity of her woe there issues a music of expression."[25] It seemed that Emily had read the fragment poems in Blackwood's and decided she too would attempts her own fragments, which she achieved with great success.

Patrick Bronte, Emily's father, had also been an enthusiastic writer and had acquired a good literary collection for his library, which was readily available for his children to draw on, confirmed by the frequent annotation in many of the books. The books recorded in Chapter one indicated that Patrick Bronte may have been interested in the German Romantic poets as well as Emily. Either that, or Emily had persuaded her father to purchase *The Works of Schiller* and other German literary works and dictionaries. From Mrs Gaskell we had learned that Emily had been learning German.

One could imagine Emily and her father (like the Rivers family in *Jane Eyre*) reading *Blackwoods's* or *The Works of Schiller*. John Hewish stated how Patrick Bronte enjoyed the company of his children around him when reading the local papers, "And with what breathless anxiety we listened, as one by one they [topics] were disclosed and explained and argued upon so ably and so well..."[26]

But it was Brussels which changed the life of Emily for the short time she was there. Robert K. Wallace had written about her Brussels trip as a great adventure into the unknown, as Emily's focus on the inner life, her visions and imagination was to find an affinity with Beethoven, as Goethe had before her. Both artists viewed nature with the same intensity and perspective. It was to change and deepen her imagination for the remainder of her short life. Like the German Romantic poets, music was an important and necessary ingredient of her poetry, and the opportunity to hear the symphonies of Beethoven would have been a great inspiration to her. Goethe remarked of Beethoven, "his talent amazes me...He is, no doubt, quite right in finding the world detestable."[27]

Imagination was another common factor between poet and composer, as Beethoven had "Excelled in the play of his imagination, the energy of his rhythm, his ardour and his control of the mighty impulses which he released."[28] Such passionate and musical emotion stayed with Emily when she arrived home with new music books, piano and fresh intensity to her poetry. In his discussion about musicians and poets, Romain Rolland commented that "Those who are only musicians, those who are only poets, are but minor princes, whose powers do not extend beyond the borders of their little provinces. But Goethe and Beethoven are emperors of the whole universe."[29]

Chapter three examined the poetry of the German Romantic poets alongside that of Emily Bronte, where the main themes of life, death, and man's place in the universe were questioned. It was there that the influences of Romanticism and the Gothic could clearly be seen. The German Romantics demonstrated how the imagination embraced and spiritualised the world, and showed how nature would be *the* leading element. The subject matter adopted by Novalis was reflected in the poetry of Emily Bronte, with its fascination with the night, its visions and spiritual aspects. Both poets looked for death and eternity in their highly symbolic poems. Goethe captured the essence of man's role in nature in his musical poetry, and its addition of Gothic machinery in such poems as the *Elf King* (*Erlköng*) and *Welcome and Farewell* (*Wilkommen und Abschied*) which had formative links with Emily 's Gondal poems, with their high emotional and musical rhythms. Novalis commented that "One remarkable characteristic of Goethe's is evident from the way he connects small insignificant incidents with more important events. He seems to have no other intention than to find a poetic way of engaging the imagination in a mysterious kind of play. Here too this rare man has caught the scent of nature's way, and learned from her a pretty trick of art. Ordinary life is full of similar accidents. They constitute a kind of play, which like all play, ends in surprise and illusion."[30]

Schiller, the well-published German Romantic poet and writer, whose books were to be found on the Bronte bookshelves, and who was frequently to be read in

Blackwood's Edinburgh Magazine, was a close friend of Goethe's, and together were the recognised leaders of the German Romantic Movement. Schiller produced many ballad-style poems as well as experimenting with the fragment poems. He often incorporated a philosophical or moral idea into his lyric poetry in his striving for knowledge about man and the universe. Tieck was also published in England and was one of the "Most influential writers of his time, a friend of numerous great contemporaries, editor of other writers' works, theatre director, playwright, novelist, poet and author of short stories."[31] His influence was characterised by an "Almost unbridled imagination…with a penchant for the uncanny," the uncanny, the strange, unnatural or eerie, was a firm feature of the Gothic, and one employed by Emily in many of her Gondal poems; "The full moon sailed bright through that Ocean on high/And the wind murmured past with a wild eerie sound."[32]

Eichendorff's portrayal of the natural world was very reminiscent of Emily 's with its aesthetic landscapes, colourful images, and the wandering poet (that ever-Romantic figure who appears in Emily's poems). Both poets portrayed nature as eternal and immortal, thus in Emily's *No Coward Soul is Mine*

Though Earth and moon were gone

And suns and universes ceased to be

And thou wert left alone

Every Existence would exist in thee.[33]

Despite the differences in country and culture, the poetry and fiction of the German Romantics did have an affinity with that of Emily Bronte. The literature shows the relationship between the poets and writers, both male and female and the discourse of the age. The analysis has proved that the German Romantic Movement was firmly established in England at the time EmilyBronte was writing. It has also provided evidence of strong similarities of interest between poets such as Goethe and Beethoven, Emily Bronte and Beethoven, nature and the Gothic. The images and spiritual visions of Novalis were also very important, being shared by Emily Bronte. One particular aspect that had been overlooked by critics of Emily Bronte was in the fragment poems, which had been introduced into England by the German Romantic poets. Emily had obviously read such poems and decided to experiment with the form, which could often be seen in anthologies of her work. Then there are the books owned by the Bronte family, containing German language and literary texts, providing another strong link.

The conclusion must be that whilst no single definitive factor links her directly to the German poets, it would be correct to accept that the German influence was present and cannot be denied. Finally, Romer Wilson, in 1929, commented on the death and subsequent loss of many of Emily's manuscripts, stating, "This is all a terrible tragedy. I cannot help it, Emily's life was one of the most terrible tragedies on earth."[34]

I am sure many people would agree with those words.

NOTES TO CHAPTERS

INTRODUCTION:

1. Holstein, Stael, Madame de, *The Influence of Literature –Upon- Society*, volume; 2 (Boston: W. Wells and T.B Waite and Co, 1813), p.12

2. Holstein, Stael, p.7

3. Ingham, Patricia, *The Brontes (*Oxford: Oxford University Press, 2008*)*, (p.225)

4. Lilian R. Furst, *Romanticism in Perspective* (London: Macmillan, 1969), p.51

5. *V. Stockley, German Literature as Known in England 1750-1800* (London: George Routledge, 1929), p.13

6. Charles Simpson, *Emily Bronte* (London: Country Life, 1929), p.114

7. Simpson, p.86

8. A. Mary F. Robinson, *Emily Bronte*, (Boston: Roberts Brothers, 1883) p.60

9. Robinson, p.60

10. Robert K, Wallace, *Emily Bronte and Beethoven* (Athens: University of Georgia

Press, 1986), p.165

11. John Hewish, *Emily Bronte: A Critical and Biographical Study* (London: Macmillan, 1969), p.125

12. Shorter, Clement, *The Complete Poems of Emily Bronte,* Introduction.

13. Rictor Norton, *Gothic Readings: The First Wave 1764-1840* (London: Leicester   University, 2000),

p.vii

14. Kenneth Clarke, *The Gothic Revival* (London: John Murray, 1962), p.111

15. Fred Botting, *Gothic* (London: Routledge, 2002), p.5

16. Botting, p.93

CHAPTER ONE:

A Literary Background

1. *The Brontë's: Then And Now*, (Haworth: The Bronte Society, 1947), p.36

2. Gaskell, E, *The Life of Charlotte Bronte* (London; J.M.Dent, 1946), p.97-8

3. Gaskell, p.98

4. Gaskell, p.100

5. Peel, Frank, in Scruton, W, *The Brontes*, p.116

6. Senior, James, *Patrick Bronte*, (U.S.A, Boston:The Stratford Company, 1921), p.14

7. Senior, p.24

8. Senior, p.53

9. Senior, p.54

10. Knapp, Bettina, L, *The Brontes* (New York: Continuum, 1992),p.21

11. *Companion to The Brontë's*, p.115

12. Clement Shorter, p.63

13. Peel, p.120

14. Peel, p.122

15. Bronte, Charlotte, *Jane Eyre*, Preface.

16. Edgerley, Mabel, C, *Then & Now*, p.50

17. Bronte, Ann, Agnes Grey, p.160

18. Agnes Grey, p.10

19. Agnes Grey, p.143

20. Bronte, Ann, *Tenant of Wildfell Hall*, Preface.

21. Bronte, Ann, Preface.

22. Knapp, *The Brontë's*, p.67

23. Knapp, p.68

24. Du Maurier, p.230

25.Wilson, Romer, *All Alone: The Life and Private History of Emily Jane Bronte* (London: Endeavour Press Ltd, 2015), p.4124

26.Wilson, p.1655

27. Radcliffe, Ann, *A Journey Made in the Summer of 1794, Through Holland and the Western Frontier of Germany, with a Return Down the Rhine to which Are Added Observations During a Tour to the Lakes of Lancashire, Westmoreland and Cumberland.* (Dublin: Wogan, p, Byrne, C, Porter Jones Rice, J, Fitzpatrick and Folingsby, G, 1795)

28. Radcliffe, p.234

29. Tompkins, J, M.S, p.250

30. Austen, Jane, *Northanger Abbey* (London: Penguin, 1995) p.47

31. Lewis, M, G, *The Monk* (Mineola, New York: Dover Publications, 2003), p.iv

32. Lewis, p.102

33. Lewis, p.94

34. Clayre, Alasdaire, *Nature and Industrialization*, (Oxford; The Open University Press, 1977), p.222

35 Maturin, Charles, *Melmoth the Wanderer* (London: Penguin Books, 1984), p.697

36 Maturin, p.150

37 Maturin, p.15-16

38 Wu, Duncan, *Romanticism: An Anthology* (Oxford: Blackwell, 1994), p.32

39 Wu, p.32

40. Wu, p.115

41.Bygrave, Stephen, *Romantic Writings* (London: The Open University/Routledge, 1996), p.280

Chapter Two:

Emily: Poetry, Themes and Influences

1. Ingham, Patricia, *The Brontes, Authors in Context* (Oxford: Oxford University Press, 2008), p.59

2.Arthur Pollard, p.53

3. A. Mary F Robinson, 57

4. Wood. H.G (Maurice), p.19

5. *Cambridge Guide to Literature in English*, 615

6. (https://www.thes.net/links2)

7. (kleurrijksisters.blogspot.co.uk/2010/07/title-cat-author-emily-.html)

8. Gerin, p,115

9. Gerin, p.116

10. Gaskell, E, *The Life of Charlotte Bronte* (London: Smith, Elder and Co.,1895), p.98

11. Gaskell, (1895) p.88

12. Shorter, p.298

13. Shorter, p.291

14. Knapp, *The Brontes*, p.39

15. A, Mary. F, Robinson, p.31

16. A, Mary, F, Robinson, p.33

17. Mrs Gaskell, *The Life of Charlotte Bronte* (London: J.M Dent, 1946), p.90

18. Shorter, Clement, *The Brontë's: Life and Letters* (London: Hodder and Staughton, 1908), p.103

19. A. Mary F. Robinson, p.18

20. James Fotheringham, *Society Transactions*, Volume 12, Part XL (Haworth: Publishing, 1906), p.110

21. Irene Tayler, *Holy Ghosts: The Male Muses of Charlotte and Emily Bronte* (New

   York: Columbia University Press, 1999), p.13

22. C. P Magill, *The Male Muses of Charlotte and Emily* Bronte (New York: Columbia University Press, 1999), p.13

23. Lucasta Miller, *The Bronte Myth* (London: Vintage, 2002), p.3

24. Tom Winifrith and Edward Chitham, *Charlotte and Emily Bronte: Literary Lives* (London: Macmillan, 1989), p.55

25. John Hewish, p.126

26. Mrs Gaskell, (1946), p.37

27. Mrs Gaskell, p.90

28. Mrs Gaskell, p.176

29. Shorter, Clement, p.231

30. F.W. Stokoe, *German Influence in the English Romantic Period 1788-1818* (Cambridge: Cambridge University /Press, 1926), p.175

31. Stokoe, p.79

32. Hewish, p.79

33. Margaret Drabble, (ed.,) *Oxford Companion to English Literature* (Oxford: Oxford University Press, 1985), p.604

34. Mrs Gaskell, p.198

35. Gezari, Janet, *Emily Jane Bronte: The Complete Poems* (London: Penguin, 1992), p.36

36. Mrs Gaskell, p.3

37. Kathleen M Wheeler, *German Aesthetic and Literary Criticism: The Romantic Ironists and Goethe*

(Cambridge: Cambridge University Press, 1984), p.87

38. *Cambridge Guide to English Literature*, p.190

39 Miriam Allott, *On Charlotte, Emily and Anne Bronte: The Critical Heritage* (London: Routledge and Keegan Paul, 1974), p.455-7

40. Bayard Quincy Morgan and A. R Hohfeld, *German Literature in Magazines 1750-1860* (Madison: Wisconsin: Wisconsin University Press, 1949), p.52

41. Mark Kipperman, p.6

42. *Encarta World Dictionary* (London: Bloomsbury, 1999), p.808

43. Rictor Norton, p.vii

44. Lucasta Miller, p.182

45. Barbara and Gareth Lloyd Evans, *The Everyman's Companion to the Brontë's* (London: J.M Dent and Sons Ltd, 1982), p.226-232

46. Margaret Lane, *The Drug-like Bronte Dream* (London: John Murray, 1980), p.65

47. Lilian R, Furst, p.84

48. John Fiske, *Myths and Myth-Makers* (London: Random House, 1996), p.17

49. James Boyd, *Notes to Goethe's Poems, Volume 1: 1749-1986* (Oxford: Basil Blackwell, 1966), p.173

50. Gezari, p.121

51. Gezari, p.174

52. Gezari, p.126

53. Gezari, p.97

54. Miller, Lucasta,, p.

55. John Hewish, p.30

56. John Hewish, p.76

57. Gezari, p.51

58. Vivien Folkenflik, *Major Writings of Germain de Stael*, (New York; Columbia University Press, 1987) p.175

59. Gezari, p.14

60. Gezari, p.7

61. Gezari, p.27

62. Gezari, p.165

63. Gezari, p.74

64. Gezari, p.51

65. Gezari, p.218

66. Sergio O Prokofieff, *Hymns to the Night* (London: Temple Lodge, 2001)

67. Gezari, p.19

68. Irene Tayler, p.300

69. Gezari, p.155

70. Gezari, p.120

71. Gezari, p.68

72. Evans, p.236

73. Lilian Furst, *Romanticism in Perspective*, p.197

74. Stevie Davies, *Emily Bronte: Heretic* (London: The Women's Press, 1994), p.57

75. Lilian Furst, p.83

76. Lilian Furst, p.89

77. Rupert Christiansan, *Romantic Affinities* (London: Penguin, 1988), p.76

78. Lilian Furst, *The Critical Idiom*, p.47

79. Hough, Graham, *The Romantic Poets* (London: Arrow Books, 1958), p.81

80. Renwick, p.154

81. Renwick, p.155

82. Renwick, p.171

83. Christiensen, p.153

84. Christiensen, p.154

85. Saintsbury, George, p.196

86. Lord David Cecil, p.7

87. Cecil, p.28

88. Paul Hamilton, *Cambridge Companion to Wordsworth* (C.U.P, 2003), P.213

89. Cecil, p.28

90. Christiensen, p.27

91. Charles Simpson, p.144

92. Gezari, p.86

93. Eddie Flintoff, *In the Steps of the Brontë's'* (Berkshire: Countryside Books, 1993), p.130

94. Gezari, p.198

95. Muriel Spark and Derek Standford, *Emily Bronte: Her Life and Work* (London: Peter Owen, 1960), p.162

96. Gezari, p.56

97. Gezari, p.73

98. Simpson, p.114

99. Herold, Christopher, J, *Mistress To An Age: A Life of Madame De Stael* (London: Readers Union, 1960), p.255

100. Mason, Daniel, Gregory, *The Romantic Composers* (London: Macmillan and Company, Ltd, 1906), p.29

101. Mason, p.33

102. Mason, p.35

103. Stevie Davies, p.51

104. Robert K Wallace, *Emily Bronte and Beethoven: Romantic Equilibrium in Fiction and Music* (Athens and London: University of Georgia Press, 1986), p.1

105. Wallace, p.2

106. Simpson, p.145

107. Wallace, p.168

108. Wallace, p.104

109. Simpson, p.149

110. Roper, p.32

111. Roper, p.47

112. Roper, p.61

113. Roper, p.221

114. Roper, p.81

115. Roper, p.67

116. Roper, p.58

117. Roper, p.1

118. Roper, 107

119. Winifred Gerin, *Emily Bronte* (Oxford: Clarendon Press, 1971), p.40

120. Robert K Wallace, p.159

121. Robert K Wallace, p.9

CHAPTER THREE

The German Romantics: Poetry

1. L.A. Willoughby, *The Romantic Movement in Germany* (London: Oxford University Press, 1930), p.3

2. Berlin, p.29

3. Berlin, p.30

4. Botting, p.5

5. Norton, p.vii

6. Willoughby, p.7

7. C.P.Magill, p.78

8. George Sampson, p.696

9. Posgate, p.146

10. Posgate, p.117

11. Posgate, p.123

12. Posgate, p.122

13. Robin Gilmour, p.27

14. Mark Kipperman, p.62

15. Mark Kipperman, p.63

16. T.W. Ward, p.109

17. Rictor Norton, p.32-9

18. Margaret Drabble, p.212

19. Kathleen Wheeler, p.

20. Penelope Fitzgerald, p.46

21. Fitzgerald, p.46

22. Osman Durrani, p.101

23. Prokoffiev, p.4

24. Prokoffiev, p.9

25. Prokoffiev, p.10

26. Prokof, p.11

27. Gezari, p.5

28. Ernest Bernbaum, *Guide Through the Romantic Movement* (New York: Ronald Press Company, 1930), p.6-10

29. Lilian R. Furst, *Romanticism in Perspective*, p.36

30. Sergio O Prokofieff, *Novalis: Hymns to the Night* (London: Temple Lodge, 2001)

31. Nicholas Saul, *History and Poetry in Novalis and in the Tradition of the German Enlightenment* (London: Institute of Germanic Studies, 1984), p.72-85

32. Prokofieff, p.4

33. Prokofieff, p.21

34. Prokofieff, p.21

35. Prokofieff, p.20

36. Prokofieff, p.20

37. Prokofieff, p.22

38.Nicholas Saul, p.143

39. D.J.Enright, *Oxford Book of Death*, p.168

40. Kathleen Wheeler, p.85

41. Gezari, p.7

42. Hughes, p.72

43. Appelbaum, p.xiii

44. Blamires, p.20

45. Blamires, p.21

46. Rolland, p.5

47. Rolland, p.6

48. Appelbaum, p.3

49. Gode, p.73

50. Gezari, p.5

51. Prokoff, p.20

52. Appelbaum, p.26

53. Gezari, p.12

54. Hardin, p.314

55. Hardin, p.316

56. Appelbaum, p.81

57. Hardin, p.63

58. Garland, p.84

59. Hardin, p.63

60. Hughes, p.110

61. Hughes, p.42

62. J.W. Thomas, p.99

63. Gezzari, p.117

64. Appelbaum, p.115

65. Hughes, p.111

66. Appelbaum, p.89

67. Gezzari, p.75

68. Gezzari, p.79

69. Hughes, p.87

70. Hughes, p.89

71. J.B Priestley, p.100

72. Willoughby, p.168

73. C.P Magill, p.76

74. Romain Rolland

75. Willoughby, p.166

76. Boyd, p.175

77. Hardin, p.314

78. Appelbaum, p.79

79. Hardin, p.64

80. Gode, p.157

81. Appelbaum, p.90

82. Appelbaum, p.95

83. Prokoffief, p.20

84. Kathleen Wheeler, p.93

85. Eliza Buckminster Lee, *Life of Jean Paul Friedrich Richter* (U.S.A: Boston: Charles C. Little and James Brown, 1982)

86. Buckminster Lee, p.29

87. Buckminster Lee, p.48-9

88. *The Dublin Penny Journal* (June, 1833) (http://www.jstor.org/stable/30002801)

Chapter Four

The German Romantics and the Novelle

☐ Furst, Lilian, *Romanticism in Perspective*, p.36

☐ Baldick, Chris, *Concise Dictionary of Literary Terms* (Oxford: Oxford University Press, 1996), p.153

☐ Bennett, p.4

☐ Bennett, p.4

☐ Bennett, p.5

□ Bennett, p.7

□ Bennett, p.7

□ Bennett, p.8

□ Bennett, p.5

□ Bennett, p.8

□ Bennett, p.11

□ Bennett, p.11

□ Bennett, p.13

□ Bennett, p.13

□ Folkenflik, Vivian, *Major Writings of Germaine de Stael* (New York, Columbia University Press, 1987), p.298

□ Goethe, J.W, *Sorrows of Young Werther* (Surrey:Oneworld Classics, Ltd.,2011), p.28

□ Goethe, p.51

□ Goethe, p.53

□ Goethe, p.53

□ Goethe, p.111

□ Mann, p.5

□ Mann, p.10

□ Mann, 11

□ Mann, p.23

□ Mann, p.36

□ Maas, Joachim, p.262

□ Carlyle, p.509

□ Carlyle, p.509

□ Carlyle, p.520

□ Carlyle, p.524

□ Carlyle, p.526

- Carlyle, p.526

- Carlyle, p.527

- Fife, Herdon Robert, *Jean Paul Friedrich Richter and E.T.A Hoffmann* (PMLA Journal, volume 22;No,1, 1907 (http://www.jstor.org/stable456660)

- Fife, p.5

- Fife, p.8

- Fife, p.5

- Fife, p.8

- Fife, p.9

- Fife, p.12

- Fife, p.31

- Fife, p.2

- Hoffmann, ET.A, *The Life and Opinions of Tom Cat Murr* (Harmondsworth: Penguin, 1999), Introduction

- Collins, George, Stuart, *Selections from the Works of Jean Paul Friedrich Richter*, p.12

- Hardin, James and Schweitzer, Christopher (Eds.,), *Dictionary of Literary Biography, volume 90; Writers in the Age of Goethe 1789-1832* (U.S.A, Detroit: Gale Research, 1989), p.316

- Carlyle, Thomas, *German Romance; Specimens of its Chief Authors* (O.U.P, 1827), p.335

- Carlyle, p.336

- Carlyle, p.339

- Carlyle, p.343

- Carlyle, p.343

CHAPTER Five

The German Women Writers:

1. Bygrave, Stephen, (ed.), *Romantic Writings* (London: Routledge/Open University, 1996), p.183

2. Brown, Hilary (ed.), *Landmarks in German Women's Writing* (Oxford: Peter Lang, 2007), p.61

3. Goodman, K.R, and Walstein, E, *The Shadow of Olympus: German Women Writers Around 1800* (U.S.A: State University of New York Press, 1992), p.17

4. Goodman and Walstein, p.22

5. Todd Kontje, *Women, the Novel, and the German Nation* (Cambridge: Cambridge University Press, 1998), p.7

6. Diethe, C, *Towards Emancipation: German Women Writers of the Nineteenth Century* (New York & Oxford: Berghahn Books, 1998), introduction

7. Diethe, p.68

8. Tymms, Marion, *The Wild Muse* (U.K., Cirencester: Memoirs Publishing, 2013), Introduction

9. Tymms, Marion, p.231

10. Bennett, E.K, *A History of the German Novelle* (Cambridge: Cambridge University Press, 1949) p.129

11. Bennett, p.130

12. Eckelmann, Dr, E.O, *Die Judenbuche* (Oxford: Oxford University Press, 1910)

13. Bennett, p.134

14. Mathieu, G, and Stern, G, (Eds,) *Introduction to German Poetry: A Dual Language Book* (New York: Dover Publications, 1991) p.83

15. Hilger, S. M, *Gender and Genre: German Women Write the French Revolution* (U.S.A: Bowman and Littlefield, University of Delaware Press, 2014) p.46

16. Kontje, p.77

17.Fetting,Friedrich, *Eine sozial-und literaturgeschicht liche Untersuchung zur deutschen Romanschriftstellerin um 1800* (Munich:Fink, 1992) p.73

18. Blackwell. J, and Zantop, S, *Bitter Healing: German Women Writers 1700-1830* (U.S.A: University of Nebraska Press, 1990), p.204

19. Blackwell, p.196

20. Goodman, K.R and Waldstein, E,

21. Blackwell, p.205

22. Goodman, p.193

23. Dawson, Ruth, *The Contested Quilt: Literature by Women in Germany 1770-1800* (London: Associated University Presses,1991), p.338

24. Dawson, p.338

25. Blackwell, p.433

26. Diethe, p.43

27. Goodman, p.97

28. Diethe, p.41

29. Brown, p.70

30. Stahl, E.L and Yuill, W.E, *German Literature in the 18th and 19th Centuries* (London: Cresst Press, 1970), p.120

31. Goodman, P.99

32. Goodman, p.100

33. Brown, p.74

34. Diethe, p.45

35. Diethe, P.51

36. Paley, David, *150 German Poems* (www.poemswithoutfrontiers.com2015

CHAPTER six

Wuthering Heights

1.Chris Baldick, *Oxford Concise Dictionary of Literary Terms* (Oxford: Oxford University Press, 1996p.152

2.Chris Baldick, p.171

3. Evans, Barbara and Gareth Lloyd, *Companion to the Brontë's* (London and Melbourne: J. M.Dent and Sons Ltd,1985), p.123

4. Senior, James, p.2

5. Reid,Weimyss, *Here and Now*, p.37

6. Charles Simpson, p.177

7. Gerin, p.212

8. *Here and Now*, p.32

9. Dunn, J, *Wuthering Heights*, *Norton Critical Edition*, (London, New York; 1991) preface

10. Dunn, J, p.314

11. Dunn, J, p.354

12. Dunn, J, p.36

13. Miller, p.171

14. Miller, p.174

15. Miller, p.172

16. Simpson, Charles, p.177

17. Spark,/Stanford p114

18. Spark/Stanford, p.116

19. Miller p.205

20. A. Mary, K, Robinson, p.20

21. Spark/Stanford, p.201

22. *Wuthering Heights*; p.141

23. *Wuthering Heights*; p.58

24. Mary, F, Robinson, p.58

25. E.M.Forster, *Aspects of the Novel*, (Harmondsworth: Penguin Books, 1964), p.149

26. Dunn, J, p.357

27. *Wuthering Heights,* p.30

28. Gerin, Winifred, p.226

29. *Wuthering Heights*, Preface

30. Du Maurier, Daphne, *The Infernal World of Branwell Brontë*, (Harmondsworth, Penguin Books, 1981), p. 94

31. Du Maurier, p.95

32. Du /Maurier, p.178

33. Robinson, p.58

34. *Wuthering Heights*, p.20

35. *Wuthering Heights*, p.61

36. Robinson, p.59

37. Robinson, p.59

38. *Wuthering Heights*, p.117

39. Du Maurier, p.208

40. Robinson, p.18

41. *Wuthering Heights*, p.130

42. *Wuthering Heights*, p.247

43. Davenport-Hines, Richard, *Gothic*, (New York: Northpoint Press, 1999) p.231

44. Hines, p.229

45. Hines, p.229

46. *Wuthering Heights*, p.252

47. *Wuthering Heights*, p.314

48. Spark/Stanford, p.114

49. Hoffmann, p.193

50. Romer Wilson, p.3534

51. Hoffmann, p.241

52. Hoffmann, p.197

53. Wilson, Romer, p.3556

54. Wilson, p.3564

55. Hoffmann, p.224

56. Romer Wilson, p.4018

CONCLUSION

1. Dobrée, Bonamy, Professor, *The Victorians and After 1830- 1914* (Volume IV) (London: Cresset Press, 1950), p.56

2. Simpson, p.48

3. Kipperman, p.7

4. Kipperman, p.14

5. Kipperman, p.73

6. Simpson, p.88

7. Tegai Hughes, p.67

8. Pykett, p.46

9. Gezari, p.7

10. Spark, p.201

11. *Blackwoods Edinburgh Magazine* (volume 53:330, April 1843), p.439

12. Tegai Hughes, p.78

13. Tegai Hughes, p.64

14. Tegai Hughes, p.65

15. Gezari, p.73

16. Gezari, p.73

17. Gezari, p.75,

18. *Blackwoods Edinburgh Magazine* (volume 82:501, July 1857), p.89

19. Hewish, p.27

20. Rolland, p.52

21. Rolland, p.77

22. Rolland, p.157

23. Wheeler, p.87

24. Appelbaum, p.xvii

25. Gezari, p.82

26. Gezari, p.182

27. Wilson, Romer, p.3491

INDEX

Germany

Hegel, 84, 103.

Herder, 103, 115,

Holderlin, 84, 103.

Huber, Therese

Hulshoff-Droste, Annette, von, 119, 121-125.

Jean Paul, 22, 71, 99-102

Kant, 56, 77, 84-85, 92, 102, 103, 108, 110, 112, 117.

Kleist, 103-110, 124

Mendelsohn, 98.

Mozart, 27, 97-98

Naubert, Benedict, 120, 128-129

Novalis, 51, 56, 63-65, 87-89, 90-99, 117.

Schiller, *22*, 35, 53-58, 75, 80, 85, 92, 94, 103, 113-117, 127, 153, 156, 162-166

Schelling, 57, 69, 84-5, 103, 160, 162.

Schlegel, A, 53, 57, 103, 117.

Schlegel, F, 53, 84, 103-104, 117, 121, 132.

Schopenhauer, Johana, 134-135.

Schubert, 96.

Schumann, 96.

Smith, Charlotte, 35-37.

Strauss, 94, 98.

Tieck, 12, 80, 93-98, 103, 105, 113, 114, 116, 117, 166

Turner, 47.

Varnhagen, von, Rahel, 135.

Wilson, Romer, 28, 153, 155, 167

Wolf, 96.

BIBLIOGRAPHY

PRIMARY SOURCES:

Appelbaum, Stanley, *Great German Poems of the Romantic Era* (New York: Dover Publications, 1995)

Dunn, J (ed.) *Wuthering Heights* (New York & London: W. W. Norton & Company, 1991)

Gezari, Janet, *Emily Jane Bronte: The Complete Poems* (London: Penguin, 1992)

Mathieu, Gustave, and Sterne, Guy, *Introduction to German Poetry* (New York: Dover Publications, 1991)

Roper, Derek, and Chitham, Edward (Eds,), *The Poems of Emily Bronte* (London: Clarendon Press, 1996)

Shorter, Clement, King, *The Complete Poems of Emily Bronte* from 1908 Edition (U.S.A: Createspace Independent Publishing Platform, 2016))

SECONDARY SOURCES

Abrams, M, H, *The Mirror and the Lamp: Romantic Theory and the Critical Tradition* (Oxford: Oxford University Press, 1953)

Allott, Miriam, *On Charlotte, Emily and Anne Bronte: The Critical Heritage* (London: Routledge and Kegan Paul, 1974)

Ameriks, Karl, *The Cambridge Companion to German Idealism* (Cambridge: Cambridge University Press, 2000)

Baldick, Chris, *Oxford Concise Dictionary of Literary Terms* (Oxford & New York: Oxford University Press, 1996)

Barker, Juliet, *The Brontes* (London: Weidenfeld and Nicholson, 1994)

Bennett, E.K, *A History of the German Novelle* (Cambridge: Cambridge University Press, 1949)

Bernbaum, Ernest, *Guide through the Romantic Movement* (New York: Ronald Press Company, 1930) Blackall, E.A, *The Novels of the German Romantics* (New York & London: Cornell University Press, 1983)

Birell, Augustine, *Life of Charlotte Bronte* (London; Walter Scott;, 1887)

Blackwell, J, & Zantop, S, *Bitter Healing: German Writers 1700-1830* (U.S.A: University of Nebraska Press, 1990)

Blamires, Harry, *The Age of Romantic Literature* (Essex: Longman, 1990)

Botting, Fred, *Gothic* (London: Routledge, 2002)

Boyd, James, *Notes to Goethe's Poems 1749-1786* (Oxford: Blackwell, 1966)

Bristow, Joseph (ed.,) *Victorian Women Poets* (Hampshire: Macmillan Press, Ltd., 1995)

Bronte, Anne, *Agnes Grey*, (Hertfordshire: Wordsworth Editions, 1998)

Bronte, Anne, *The Tenant of Wildfell Hall*, (Harmondsworth, Penguin Group, 1994)

Bronte, Charlotte, *Emma* (London; J.M. Dent and Sons, Ltd, 1980)

Bronte, Charlotte, *Jane Eyre* (Harmondsworth; Penguin Classics, 1994)

Bronte, Charlotte, *Shirley* (Hertfordshire; Wordsworth Editions, 1993)

Bronte, Charlotte, *The Professor* (London; Thomas Nelson And Sons Ltd.,circa 1950 (undated)

,Bronte Charlotte, *Villette* (London; Smith, Elder, and Co., 1896)

Society Transactions, Volume 12, Part XL (Haworth: Publishing, 1906)

Brown, Hilary (ed.,), *Landmarks in German Women's Writing* (Switzerland: Peter Lang, 2007)

Browning, Barrett, Elizabeth, *Aurora Leigh* (London: Women's Press, 1978)

Cannon, J, *The Brontes: A Family History* (Gloucestershire: Sutton Publishing, 2007)

Chitham, Edward, *A Life of Emily Bronte* (Oxford: Blackwell, 1987)

Christiansen, Rupert, *Romantic Affinities: Portraits From An age 1780-1830* (London: Penguin, 1988),

Clarke, Kenneth, *The Gothic Revival* (London: John Murray, 1962)

Crump, R, W, *Charlotte and Emily Bronte: A Reference Guide 1916-1954* (Boston: G.K Hall, 1985)

Crump, Kenneth, *Charlotte and Emily Bronte: A Reference Guide 1955-1983* (Boston: G.K Hall, 1986)

Curran, Stuart, (Ed.), *The Cambridge Companion to British Romanticism* (Cambridge: Cambridge University Press, 1996)

Daiches, David, (Ed.), *Wuthering Heights* (Harmondsworth: Penguin, 1967)

Davies, Stevie, *Emily Bronte: Heretic* (London: The Women's Press, 1994)

Davies, Stevie, *Emily Bronte: The Artist as a Free Woman* (Manchester: Carcanet Press Limited, 1983)

Dawson, Ruth. P, *The Contested Quilt: Literature by Women in Germany 1770-1800* (London: Associated University Presses, 2002)

De Man, Paul, *Romanticism and Contemporary Criticism* (Manchester: John Hopkins University, 1997)

Diethe, Carol. *Towards Emancipation: German Women Writers of the Nineteenth Century* (Oxford & New York: Berghahn Books, 1998)

Dingle, Herbert, *The Mind of Emily* Bronte (London: Martin Brian & O'Keefe, 1974)

Drabble, Margaret, *The Oxford Companion to English Literature* (Oxford: Oxford University, 1985)

Durrani, Osman, *German Poetry of the Romantic Era* (Leamington Spa: Berg, 1986)

Eagleton, Terry, *Literary Theory: An Introduction* (London: Blackwell, 1997)

Elton, Oliver, *A Survey of English Literature 1780-1830* (London: Edward Arnold, 1920

Encarta World English Dictionary (London: Bloomsbury, 1999)

Enright, D.J, *The Oxford Book of Death* (Oxford: Oxford University Press, 1983)

Evans, Barbara and Evans, Gareth, *The Everyman's Companion to the Brontes* (London: J.M.Dent & Sons, 1985)

Fiske, John, *Myths and Myth-Makers* (London: Random House, 1996)

Fitzgerald, Penelope, *The Blue Flower* (London: Flamingo, 1996)

Flintoff, Eddie, *In the Steps of the Brontes* (Newbury: Countryside Books, 1993)

Folkenflik, Vivien (Ed.), *Major Writings of Germain de Stael* (New York: Columbia University Press, 1987)

Forster, E.M, *Aspects of the Novel* (Harmondsworth: Pelican, 1964)

Frank, Katherine, *Emily Bronte: A Chainless Soul* (London: Hamish Hamilton, 1990)

Furst, Lilian, *Romanticism in Perspective* (London: Macmillan, 1969)

Furst, Lilian, *The Contours of European Romanticism* (London: Macmillan, 1979)

Garland, H.B, *A Concise Survey of German Literature, 2nd edition* (London: Macmillan, 1976)

Gaskell, Elizabeth, *The Life of Charlotte Bronte*(London: J.M Dent, 1946)

Gerin, Winifred, *Emily Bronte* (Oxford: Oxford University Press, 1979)

Gilmour, Robin, *The Victorian Period: The Intellectual and Cultural Context of English Literature 1830-1890* (London: Longman, 1993)

Gode, Alexander, *Anthology of German Poetry through the Nineteenth Century* (New York: Fred Ungar, 1972)

Goethe, J.W, Von, *The Sorrows of Young Werther* (London: One World Classics, 2011)

Goodman, K.R, & Waldstein, E, *In the Shadow of Olympus: German Women Writers Around 1800* (U.S.A; Albany: University of New York, 1992)

Hardin, James and Schweitzer, Christopher (eds.), *Dictionary of Literary Biography, Volume 90, German Writers in the Age of Goethe; 1789-1832* (Detroit: Gale Research, 1989)

Hewish, John, *Emily Bronte: A Critical and Biographical Study* (London: Macmillan, 1969)

Hoffmann, E.T.A, *The Life and Opinions of the Tomcat Murr* (London: Penguin, 1999)

Hoffmann, E.T.A, *Tales of Hoffmann* (London: Penguin Books, 1988)

Hough, Graham, *The Romantic Poets* (London: Grey Arrow Editions, 1958)

Howells, Carol Anne, *Love, Mystery and Misery; Feeling in Gothic Fiction* (London: University of London, 1978)

Hughes, Glyn, Tegai, *Romantic German Literature* (London: Edward Arnold, 1979)

Ingham, Patricia, *The Brontë's* (Oxford: Oxford University Press, 2006)

Kipperman, Mark, *Beyond Enchantment; German Idealism and English Romantic Poetry* (Philadelphia: University of Pennsylvania Press, 1986)

Knapp, L, Bettina, *The Brontë's* (New York: Continuum Publishing Company, 1992)

Kontje, Todd, *Women, the Novel, And the German Nation* (Cambridge: Cambridge University Press, 1998)

Lane, Margaret, *The Drug-Like BronteDream* (London: John Murray, 1980)

Lemon, Charles, *Classics of Bronte Scholarship* (Haworth: Bronte Society, 1999)

Levinson, Marjorie, *The Romantic Fragment Poem* (Chapel Hill and London: The University of North Carolina Press, 1986)

Magill, C.P, *German Literature* (London: Oxford University Press, 1974)

Maurier, Daphne Du, *The Infernal World of Branwell Bronte* (Harmondsworth: Penguin, 1981)

Miller, Lucasta, *The Bronte Myth* (London: Vintage, 2002)

Morgan, Bayard, Quincey, and Hohfeld, A, R, *German Literature in Magazines 1750-1860* (Madison, Wisconsin: University of Wisconsin Press, 1974)

Norton, Rictor, *Gothic Readings; The First Wave, 1764-1840* (London: Leicester University Press, 2000)

Peck, J, & Coyle, M, *Literary Terms and Criticism* (London: Macmillan Press, 1995)

Posgate, Helen, B, *Madame, de Stael* (New York: Twayne Publishers, 1968)

Priestley, J, B, *Literature and Western Man* (London: Heinemann, 1962)

Prokofieff, Sergio, O, (Ed.), *Novalis; Hymns to the Night and Spiritual Songs* (London: Temple Lodge, 2001)

Pykett, Lyn, *Emily Bronte* (Basingstoke: Macmillan, 1989)

Ratchford, Fanny, E, *Gondal's Queen; A Novel in Verse by Emily Jane Bronte* (Austin: University of Texas Press, 1955)

Robinson, F. Mary. A, *Emily* Bronte (Boston: Roberts Brothers, 1883)

Rolland, Romain, *Goethe and Beethoven* (New York and London: Benjamin Bloom, 1968)

Sampson, George, *The Concise Cambridge History of English Literature* (Cambridge: Cambridge University Press, 1946)

Saul, Nicholas, *History and Poetry in Novalis and in the Tradition of the German Enlightenment* (London: Institute of Germanic Studies, 1984)

Scruton, William, *The Brontes* (Bradford: The Arthur Dobson Publishing Company, 1968)

Senior, James, *Patrick Bronte* (U.S.A, Boston: The Stratford Company Ltd, 1921)

Simpson, Charles, *Emily Jane Bronte* (London: Country Life, 1929)

Smith, Anne, *The Art of Emily Bronte* (London: Vision Press, 1976)

Spark, Muriel, and Stanford, Derek, *Emily Bronte; Her Life and Work* (London: Peter Owen, 1985)

Stevenson, W, H, *Emily and Anne Bronte* (London: Routledge and Kegen Paul, 1968)

Stockley, V, *German Literature As Known in England 1750-1800* (London: George Routledge, 1929)

Stokoe, F, W, *German Influence in the English Romantic Period* (New York: Russell and Russell, 1963)

Tayler, Irene, *Holy Ghosts; The Male Muses of Charlotte and Emily* Bronte(New York: Columbia University Press, 1999)

Tennyson, Alfred, Lord, *The Poems of Alfred Lord Tennyson* (London: Grant Richards, 1903)

Thomas, J, W, (Ed.), *German Verse in English Translation* (New York: Ams Press Incorporated, 1996)

Tymms, M, *The Wild Muse* (Cirencester: Memoirs Publishing, 2013)

Vanson, Frederic, *Little Poems from Novalis* (Bakewell: Hub Publications, 1975)

Vidler, Alec, R, *The Church in an Age of Revolution* (Harmonsworth; Penguin Group, 1990)

Wallace, Robert, K, *Emily Bronte and Beethoven* (Athens: University of Georgia Press, 1986)

Ward, T, W, *The English Poets, Volume IV* (London: Macmillan, 1933)

Wheeler, Kathleen, M, *German Aesthetic and Literary Criticism: The Romantic Ironists and Goethe* (Cambridge: Cambridge University Press, 1984)

White, Diana, M, *Research in Germanic Studies* (London: London University Press, 1995)

Willoughby, L, A, *The Romantic Movement in Germany* (London: Oxford University Press, 1930)

Wilshire, Bruce, *Romanticism and Evolution; The Nineteenth Century* (London: University Press of America, 1985)

Wilson, Romer, *All Alone*: *The Life and Private History Of Emily Bronte* (U.S.A: Kessinger Publishing, 2010)

Winnifrith, Tom and Chitham, Edward, *Charlotte and Emily Bronte; Literary Lives* (London: Macmillan, 1989)

Winnifrith, Tom, *The Brontë's and their Background; Romance and Reality* (London: Macmillan, 1973)

Wood, H.G, *Frederick Denison Maurice* (Cambridge; Cambridge University Press, 1950

Young, Edward, *Night Thoughts on Life, Death and Immortality* (London: J.F and C, Rivington, 1790)

FULL MANY A LAND INVITES THEE NOW...

Oh, Howarth, my Howarth
Where hast thou gone?
So foreign a flavour envelopes thee now.
I cannot return to rest my weary brow
Whilst other skies, in accents strange
Disturb my mind on overcast moorland days.
The birds muse over memories of familiar tongues
That brought warmth on a chilly morn.
Steep, cobbled streets powerlessly cling
To a brave new dawn.
Holding on fast to the rock of immortality
I watch...
From those mountains on Gondal's shore
Clinging on to noble hearts
Forever, ever more.
While all around me weeds o'er grow
And dark moss pervades the stone.
I close my eyes and indulge in memories rapturous pain.

Recalling and inviting the visionary flame
Of distant souls who penned their dreams
Bequeathing faded yesteryears in places near and far-
Gazing down now from that bright moorland star
To Nature's hybrid humanity.

Maggieallen©

www.ingramcontent.com/pod-product-compliance
Lightning Source LLC
Chambersburg PA
CBHW060502290526
45791CB00001B/228